Our Hearts Were Strangely Lukewarm

Our Hearts Were Strangely Lukewarm

The American Methodist Church and the
Struggle with White Supremacy

John Elford

Foreword by Ian Straker

WIPF & STOCK · Eugene, Oregon

OUR HEARTS WERE STRANGELY LUKEWARM
The American Methodist Church and the Struggle with White Supremacy

Wipf & Stock
An Imprint of Wipf and Stock Publishers
199 W. 8th Ave., Suite 3
Eugene, OR 97401

www.wipfandstock.com

PAPERBACK ISBN: 978-1-6667-6754-4
HARDCOVER ISBN: 978-1-6667-6755-1
EBOOK ISBN: 978-1-6667-6756-8

05/24/23

Contents

Foreword

BY THE DAWN OF the Antebellum period and spurred on by gains made during the First and Second Great Awakenings, more Americans were Methodist than any other Christian tradition. The nation's split into northern and southern factions during the Civil War had been foreshadowed by the historic, similar split of the Methodist Episcopal Church in 1844. But counted together, those two resulting main factions of American Methodism helped to define American Protestantism.

The desire to regain numerical supremacy encouraged the main branches of Methodism to work toward reunion during the first third of the twentieth century. As others have ably documented, the hope of the Methodist Church beyond numerical dominance was to assume a leading role in shaping American life and morals; with the United States seen as the world's leading Christian nation, those leading the push for Methodist unification had great hopes of having their church shape the world's future, with an impact far beyond the church's doors. As described in *Our Hearts Were Strangely Lukewarm*, reunion was achieved at the expense of African-American Methodists, who were consigned by the new church's constitution to a segregated status.

Perhaps all of those most eager to lead American culture through Methodist unification did not intend to broadcast approval of racial discrimination, but that is, in fact, what happened. The formation of the nation's largest Protestant denomination made national news, which included informing the world that the Methodist Church had baptized Jim Crow—clearly claiming compatibility between Christianity and racial segregation. As we look back today on the protests and violence associated with the modern Civil Rights Movement, we must not forget that the national membership of the Methodist Church supplied partisans on all sides of the racial strife.

It is clear in our time that the Civil Rights Movement did not settle for all time the problems of racial segregation and discrimination. The killing of unarmed African Americans by police, racially motivated mass shootings, and the continuing controversy over displaying confederate flags and monuments are just some of the most obvious indications that the United States has a long way to go in achieving justice for all, true interracial understanding and racial equality. One might reasonably expect that followers of Jesus have a role to play in nudging the nation toward harmony and equity. Although the United Methodist Church may not claim today the same percentage of the American population among its membership as its predecessor bodies did some sixty years ago, is it too much to hope that it will play an unqualified positive role in these days?

In the nineteenth century, racism was bolstered by a deluge of junk science purporting to prove that racial differences in intelligence and performance were inherent and immutable. Such ideas continued to have currency through at least the thoroughly debunked discussions of the late twentieth century about IQ tests. Scientists today are clear that there is no biological or scientific basis for race as an objective factor. Still, centuries of racial discrimination continue to give the idea of intelligence as race-based immense social, political, and economic power.

The testimony of those who have managed to extricate themselves from white supremacist and white nationalist ideologies and activities makes clear that those hateful views were based on lies and gross misinformation; key to their redemption has been confronting the unadorned truth about history and the tragic damage caused by racist actions and ideas. Surely, the way to overcome the mistakes of the past begins with a clear-eyed understanding of history and a commitment to chart a better future. This truth is no less true for the church than it is for the broader society. Individual Methodists and the church as an institution have been wrong on race in the past, and the repercussions of those errors have cost lives; it is incumbent on today's Methodists to summon the courage and sustained effort needed to face its past faults squarely as we forge a new path that is thoroughly informed by the principles that are the heart of the gospel of Jesus Christ.

Therefore it is more than timely that this book is written and read in these times. It is not just for United Methodists or even other Christians but for all who have an interest in how American ideas of race have, at times, led church people to embrace a compromised version of the faith that has had echoes heard far and wide. In 2020 the Council of Bishops of the United Methodist Church expressed its commitment to dismantling racism in the church, joining the perpetual mission of the United Methodist Commission on Religion and Race. It may be a shame that such a declaration had to follow and not precede a series of killings of unarmed African Americans that sparked international protests, but the journey to end racism requires intentional effort and must begin somewhere. The bishops demand that we move beyond prayer into action and "ask United Methodists to read all they can on the subject of anti-racism and engage in conversations with children, youth and adults."[1] Coming to grips with the church's history of complicity with racism and white supremacy is a good place to start, and thus we are fortunate to have John Elford's accessible and accurate historical overview. Perhaps an honest reckoning with the past, coupled with a firm dedication to a better future, will, at last, allow the church to truly lead this nation and the world, if not to a new heaven, at least to a new earth.

Dr. Ian Straker

1. "Council of Bishops Statement."

Acknowledgements

EVERY BOOK IS A group project, and this one is no exception. As I put the finishing touches on this book, I am profoundly aware of how I have leaned on the work of previous historians, like Peter C. Murray, Donald G. Mathews, Russell E. Richey, Kenneth E. Rowe, Jean Miller Schmidt, Frederick A. Norwood, and a host of others who have made my work easier. If I haven't gotten the history right, though, it's all on me.

In attempting to write a "short" overview, I'm also aware of how much I've had to leave out. I hope that readers will join me in filling in the rest of this history as we seek to repair the truth about ourselves and our church.

First, I'm so grateful for my wife, Linda, who read everything I wrote and coauthored all of the study questions. What a boon to have a writer and copyeditor under the same roof! She has been a rock of support, a gentle critic, and a constant source of reassurance when I was ready to throw in the towel.

Special thanks to my colleague and friend John Wright and my new friend Ian Straker, who gave invaluable time and energy to this project. Their careful scholarship helped keep my theology and history straight. This book would be so much poorer without them.

I'm also indebted to Chad Seales, Trish Merrill, Tom Downing, Tom Hatfield, David Woodruff, Joshunda Sanders, Adama Brown, Tim Anderson, and Lisa Blaylock, who read portions of the manuscript and gave thoughtful and encouraging advice.

This book is written primarily for lay people, and so I must give a shout out to so many lovely lay folks: to St. John's UMC, Austin; to the Downtowners and *Eklektikos* classes at FUMC, Austin; and to the Explorers, Wesley Plus, and Odyssey classes at University UMC, Austin. Your interest and enthusiasm helped propel me toward the finish line.

Acknowledgements

To folks who helped me understand various aspects of our Methodist racial justice work: Ed King, Sue Thrasher, Betty Brandt, Heather Hahn, Matt Johnson, Cynthia Astle, Beth McClure, Andy Stoker, Andy Lewis, Karen and John Flowers, Betty Curry, Byrd Bonner, Terrence Hays, Elaine Moy, Tyrus Sturgis, Elaine Stanovsky, and Ted Campbell. To all of you, my deepest appreciation.

To Matthew Wimer and the staff at Wipf and Stock, who worked patiently with me to produce a real, live book, praise and thanksgiving.

To my new friends in the archives: Ashley Boggan D. and Frances Lyons at the General Commission on Archives and History, huge thanks for opening up new worlds to this newbie historian.

To my church, University UMC, Austin, and Pastors Teresa Welborn, Earl Kim, and Heather Green for helping keep me sane and reminding me that life is so much more than tapping on a keyboard.

And finally, to my family—Linda, Chris, Xiaolin, Rowan, Lauren, and Brendan—for laughter, love, inspiration, and regular doses of humility throughout this time. You are the very best!

Epiphany 2023

List of Abbreviations

AME	The African Methodist Episcopal Church (1816–)
AMEZ	The African Methodist Episcopal Zion Church (1820–)
ASWPL	Association of Southern Women for the Prevention of Lynching
BMCR	Black Methodists for Church Renewal
CIC	Commission on Interracial Cooperation
CJ	Central Jurisdiction
CME	The (Colored) Christian Methodist Episcopal Church
COFO	Council of Federated Organization
CSR/LCA	Christian Social Relations and Local Church Activities
GBCS	General Board of Church and Society
GCAH	General Commission on Archives and History
EJI	Equal Justice Initiative
EUBC	The Evangelical United Brethren Church (1946–68)
GC	General Conference
GCORR	General Commission on Religion and Race
HBCU	A Historically Black College or University
HUAC	House Committee on Un-American Activities (1938–69)
IRC	Indiana Remembrance Coalition
MAMML	Mississippi Association of Methodist Ministers and Lay People

List of Abbreviations

MC	The Methodist Church (1939–68)
MEC	The Methodist Episcopal Church (1784–1939)
MECS	The Methodist Episcopal Church, South (1844–1939)
MFSA	Methodist Federation for Social Action
MPC	The Methodist Protestant Church (1830–1939)
MPH	Methodist Publishing House (1939–68)
NAACP	National Association for the Advancement of Colored People
NBEDC	National Black Economic Development Conference
SRC	Southern Regional Council
UMC	The United Methodist Church (1968–)
UMW	United Methodist Women
UPS	Union Presbyterian Seminary
UWF	United Women of Faith
WD	Woman's Division of Christian Service of the Board of Missions
WMC	Women's Missionary Council
YWCA	Young Women's Christian Association

I

Introduction

It was the end of summer 1976. My plans to become a high school teacher had shifted, and I was now heading off to seminary. Earlier that year, I'd attended an inquiry weekend at Union Theological Seminary in Richmond, Virginia (now Union Presbyterian Seminary), and I'd fallen in love with the school. The wisdom and kindness of professors, some of whom lived in houses that lined the campus, charmed me. All of the students I met had a deep passion for the church and ministry.

At that time, Union Seminary (UPS) was actually a three-school consortium: the seminary itself, the Presbyterian School of Christian Education—all White—and the School of Theology of Virginia Union University (VUU)—all Black. Students at the three schools crossed paths in the cafeteria, on campus, and sometimes in classes.

On the first day of seminary, I arrived early for breakfast and sat with some friends I had made in the dorm. I noticed that all of the White students sat together at tables scattered across the room, while all of the Black students from VUU sat crowded together around one table. Why are we sitting segregated from each other? I wondered aloud to my friends. So a couple of us picked up our trays and asked the VUU students if we could join them. We were all a bit nervous, although for different reasons. We were breaking some unwritten rule. Our Black tablemates told us later that they wondered if this was a prank—or worse.

Over time, other students joined our newly integrated table. We planned to meet together in the dorms for late-night Bible studies, attend each other's churches, and engage in conversation about the church and race. I learned that the VUU students felt safe when they were at table together. Safe from what? I wondered. Only in looking back did I become aware that they felt safe from the many ways they had been made to feel they were less in a culture dominated by White people, a culture all of us White students were inoculated with and seemed entirely unaware of.

Our new VUU friends humored us, and we kept up our conversations for a time, but soon our studies got the better of us, and we moved on to other things. At least, that was the case for the White students. The Black students still had to struggle with racism in subtle and overt ways every single day. Thanks to our White privilege, we could leave the work of building better race relations to another time and place simply because it wasn't urgent work for us. Or so we imagined.

I wonder how many of us who are White have had experiences with racism in our past that we've set aside or even forgotten because we didn't have the awareness or the framework to recognize what was really going on.

UPS had a large quadrangle with a central field where we relaxed, throwing frisbees and playing touch football. I'd made friends with Robert, a VUU student, who went on to serve in the church as a pastor. Robert and I spent time together, often riding back and forth to seminary during the holidays. He had a CB radio and taught me CB speak so that we could get up north in record time.

One day, Robert and I were running pass plays in the quad when an older woman approached us. She wanted to know the way to Ginter Park Presbyterian Church. I pointed down the road, and off she went.

Robert looked at me: "Did you notice anything unusual about that conversation?"

"Not really," I had to confess.

"When she came up to us, she addressed her question to you. She never even made eye contact with me."

At the time I brushed it off. Robert was being overly sensitive, I thought. Surely she had looked at both of us. In retrospect, I now know that he was calling my attention not just to an example of personal prejudice but to systemic racism—the ways we have internalized racism so that we don't even notice it. Racism pervades our interactions with each other in ways that consistently promote racial inequality and support White privilege.

Introduction

The Church and White Supremacy

This book is my contribution to a much-needed conversation about racism and White supremacy in the White American Methodist Church, one I wish I had begun more earnestly decades ago. I've been a United Methodist pastor for thirty years, and while I have worked on racism in bits and pieces in different churches, I didn't make a deep dive into this work until 2014, following the police shooting and murder of Michael Brown in Ferguson, Missouri.

I had just finished reading Ta-Nehisi Coates's book *Between the World and Me*. I was so convicted by his work that I extended a general invitation to the church for anyone interested to join me for a book study. More than thirty people squeezed into the parsonage living room for a lively and engaged, at times awkward and difficult conversation. Clearly what we were seeing on the evening news—the murder of young Black men at the hands of police—had struck a deep chord. We were forced to face our own prejudices and the challenge of how we might use our White privilege to work against racism as a systemic problem.

Out of that study, a small group committed to anti-racist work formed. It was intentionally a group of White folks gathered to uncover our prejudices and failings in relation to race. The group has grown over the years to include both study and action. We've read and discussed books, articles, and podcasts. But we've also joined groups like the Austin Justice Coalition in their work on the complex issues of race and policing in Austin. Scrutinizing the city budget, police training, and community policing are powerful ways to engage in reshaping systems toward more racial equity and accountability.

Over the last eight years, I've discovered that it's relatively easy to find racism out there, in the public square, and to avoid confronting the reality that racism is baked into the church itself. Through the work of scholars like Robert P. Jones and Jemar Tisby, I'm learning that the preservation of the legacy of racism in our country was not limited to small groups of Klan members, White citizen's councils, or neo-Nazis. American Christianity has played a key role in supporting a White supremacist social order. And this support has not come just from the fringes of the American church. Virtually every major mainline Protestant denomination—Methodist, Presbyterian, Disciples, Lutheran—has supported and, at times, even promoted White supremacy.

3

This is not what I learned about the mainline church in seminary. Methodists were pillars of the community. Look at our hospitals and universities. Look at our global mission and relief efforts. There is so much to be proud of in the work of our church. But we were not in the lead in denouncing racism. As a historically White denomination, Methodists in the North and South routinely dismissed calls from the national church challenging the legacy of racism.

Just to be clear, the history of the Methodist Church in America is full of exceptions to what I have just said. Abolitionists in the Methodist Church put their very lives at risk preaching against slavery in the eighteenth and nineteenth centuries. In the early twentieth century, Methodist women worked powerfully to end lynching. The national Methodist Church offered resources and concrete support for the civil rights movement of the 1960s. At every stage of our journey as a church, there were folks who held us accountable to a higher morality. In this book, we'll lift up those shining stars who illuminated the way, often at a high personal cost.

This book will follow these two streams in the Methodist Church, one working to overcome racial inequalities and White supremacy, and the other either complicit or actively transmitting the virus of anti-Black racism.[1] A full treatment of this history would move significantly beyond the scope of this book. My goal is to provide an overview of these two competing streams in our church: White American Methodists who compromised, ignored, or actively supported White supremacy and those who fought to dismantle it.

I'll be using a particular definition of *racism*. People often define racism as any prejudice against another person because of their race. Stanford psychologist Steven O. Roberts argues that racism is more than that: "Racism is a system of advantage based on race. It is a hierarchy. It is a pandemic. Racism is deeply embedded within U.S. minds and U.S. society that it is virtually impossible to escape."[2] Racism is a socially constructed system that rewards some and harms others based on race.

Sheila M. Beckford and E. Michelle Ledder helpfully refine the definition of racism further into two categories: "interpersonal racism [that] focuses on beliefs, values, and actions held within a person or expressed

1. In this book, we will focus on anti-Black racism, defined by the Movement for Black Lives as a "term used to specifically describe the unique discrimination, violence and harms imposed on and impacting Black people specifically." Quoted in Saad, *White Supremacy*, 84.

2. Feder, "Stanford Psychologist," para. 3.

within a relationship (either professional or personal)" and "institutional or systemic racism [that] focuses on policies, practices, and procedures that perpetrate racism within an institution" such as a church or a denomination. While my attention in this study will lean toward the systemic racism that we find in the church, I understand that addressing racism in the church means addressing both interpersonal and systemic racism.[3]

I'll also be using a term that has recently become more controversial, *White supremacy.* It's not a new term. In fact, in the history we'll be covering here, it's actually pretty common to find the words "White supremacy" used to defend slavery, Jim Crow laws, and segregation. White supremacy is not confined to the overt racism that characterizes the alt-right or Klan movements. White supremacy also applies to the many ways that White people and White culture are valued, often unconsciously, more than other people and cultures, just as in the incident I cited above. The woman looking for Ginter Park Presbyterian Church simply assumed that I, a White person, would be safer to ask or more likely to know the answer than my Black friend.

As you read ahead, I hope you'll hear the words White supremacy not as an insult but simply as a descriptor of our culture's operating system. In the words of Tim Wise, White supremacy is "the operationalized form of racism in the United States and throughout the Western world."[4] It's a system that all of us are born into that gives White people power and privilege, all the while harming those who are not White.[5] Since we're focusing on an institution—the church—we'll be looking more closely at how White supremacy has not only infected the church but was (and still is) carried and spread by the church like a virus.

But Why?

You've read this far, and you may be wondering, "Why?" Why drag ourselves through these awful stories about our White supremacist, proslavery origins? Wouldn't we be better served by centering our attention on those who fought for justice and equality?

I'd like to offer several reasons why I think this study of our church's difficult history with regard to race is so important. The first is a brilliant

---

3. Beckford and Ledder, *Anti-Racism 4Reals*, 106–7.

4. Wise, "Tim Wise's Definitions," para. 4.

5. See Oluo, *Talk about Race,* 12–14, for a fuller description of White supremacy.

analogy that comes from Dr. Martin Luther King Jr. In his "Letter from Birmingham Jail," King writes, "Like a boil that can never be cured as long as it is covered up but must be opened with all its ugliness to the natural medicines of air and light, injustice must be exposed, with all the tension its exposure creates, to the light of human consciences and the air of national opinion before it can be cured."[6]

When we are dealing with physical pain, we understand what this means. Only when I finally make an appointment to see the doctor and show up for physical therapy does my lower back improve. But we have a harder time understanding how this process works with psychological or moral pain. Dr. King is urging us to see that it's the same formula. We must expose the virus of racism for all that it truly is, and we must treat it so that we can be healed and whole. In order for the church to be all God calls us to be, we must reckon with our history of causing harm and suffering, with the full history of our racist past. We must confess and lament that all of this actually did happen, and then we can begin the transformational work of undoing racism in our time.

Here's the second reason. At the University of Texas, next door to University UMC where I served as senior pastor, these words from the Gospel of John are etched over the south entrance to the Main Building and Tower: "Ye shall know the truth and the truth shall make you free" (John 8:32 KJV). This is a familiar text from John's Gospel. There is freedom and liberation in knowing what really happened in our history. Yes, it's hard work. And we will uncover some very unpleasant truths. All of which led one wit to paraphrase this text: "The truth will set you free but first it will make you miserable."[7] But it also may well be the most important work we do in understanding why our world is the way it is and how it might be so much more.

Clint Smith, in his book *How the Word Is Passed*, writes about watching students in a Juneteenth presentation on Galveston Island. The students were in a summer enrichment program, and together they presented a timeline of enslaved peoples up to June 19, 1865. Smith confesses wishing that he had known this history when he was younger. He felt that he "would have been liberated from a social and emotional paralysis . . . that had arisen from never knowing enough of my own history to effectively identify the lies I was being told by others."

6. King, "Letter," para. 24.

7 Original source of this quote is unknown.

Smith recalls being taught growing up that there was something wrong with him, with Black children, and with Black communities, rather than the truth about how all of this was the result of decisions by "the powers that be" for generations. So far from taking agency away from young people, Smith argues for the enormous value there is in providing young people with the framework to understand why their society looks like it does. The key to their empowerment is "understanding that all of this was done not by accident but by design."[8] All of us, Black and White, have been disfigured by the distortions, the lies, and the pain of White supremacy. There is great liberation to be found in reckoning with our painful past.

Third, and perhaps most important, undoing racism and White supremacy is simply part of being a Christian disciple. Our anti-racist work toward equality for all is not driven by a political party platform but comes directly from God. It's rooted in the belief that God's intention for the world is justice and peace. Jesus's first sermon (Luke 4:18–19) makes it plain that God is on the side of broken and oppressed people. How, then, can the ministry of the church be anything less than liberating those who have been oppressed by White supremacy and racism?

Finally, allow me to add why I, an older White male, am doing this work. When we first began working on anti-racism at University Church, we'd have folks who joined us for a short time and then left the group because we were not racially diverse. They wanted to work on racism with people of color.

Over the last few years, I've learned that there are different but equally crucial anti-racism projects. There are groups like "One World" and "Undoing Racism" that intentionally bring together White, Black, and Latinx folks to study and work together on our racial history and becoming anti-racist. Having persons of color in the room provides almost immediate feedback on our work. It helps us stay focused on the overwhelming systems that support White supremacy in which we are enmeshed. It provides immediate accountability when we say we are against racism but are not involved in any substantive way in undoing racism.

But here's the thing—undoing racism is not up to people of color. It's not their responsibility to take on the burden of guiding White people into the light. Facing White supremacy in the Methodist Church must be the work of White Methodists. White supremacy was created over decades, centuries even, by White people to maintain the supremacy of White

8. Smith, *How the Word*, 178–81.

people. And so it makes sense that in order to undo White supremacy, we White Methodists need to do our work together to understand, for example, how our own internalized White privilege works. How the deck is stacked against folks who are not White from the get-go. How we may have been part of maintaining White supremacy in our churches. And once we begin to become aware of that privilege, we can take on the work of dismantling it.

This difficult, uncomfortable work is also necessary for our healing and our truth-telling. And it's work that White pastors and lay leaders in the United Methodist Church (UMC) must take on if we truly desire a world that more closely reflects the reign of God.

Since this book is centered on uncovering the myriad ways the Methodist Church has supported White supremacy, the focus will be on White people. I hope that every reader understands that the anti-racist work of Black people at each stage of history was critical. In most cases, it was decisive, and it showed a resilience and prophetic courage worthy of emulation. This book focuses somewhat narrowly on White Methodism—both the good and the bad—not to exclude anyone but because White people bear most of the responsibility in the work of undoing anti-Black racism. Throughout the book, I will lift up some of the stirring figures in the Black Methodist Church. For those interested in diving in deeper, I commend to you *Black People in the Methodist Church* by William B. McClain or J. H. Graham's *Black United Methodists*.

We'll approach our subject chronologically, beginning with John Wesley and his work against slavery. Next, we pick up with Methodists in America and how the church came to separate over slavery in 1844. Chapter 4 follows the northern and southern Methodist churches through Reconstruction to their union in 1939. In chapters 5 and 6, we'll look more closely at how the church both supported and fought against segregation and White supremacy in the civil rights movement of the 1950s and 1960s. And we'll conclude with the larger church's reckoning with racism in our own time in chapters 7 and 8.

Before we jump in, a few final considerations. The first is about language and terminology. The old language of "slaves" and "slaveholders" has been replaced by new language that seeks to honor the humanity of the persons who were enslaved. I'll use language like "enslaved" and "enslavers" to honor those whose lives could never be fully owned by anyone.

The second is about slavery. I want to be very clear that when I write about slavery as an institution or as a system, there should be an asterisk. It's not simply an institution like a school or health care system. It's a brutal system where human beings were reduced to property. It's a system where families were separated, women were raped, and men were tortured and dismembered. It's a system of violence and terror that ought to have provoked the highest forms of moral revulsion, especially from the church.

A conversation that Clint Smith records drove this point home for me. He was interviewing John Cummings at the Whitney Plantation in Wallace, Louisiana. The museum there was founded by Cummings, a wealthy trial lawyer from New Orleans. He told Smith that as he began to read documents about the history of the plantation, he was led deeper into a study of slavery. Since then, he has read about eleven hundred oral histories of enslaved persons. While reading them, he thought, "sooner or later I'm going to get to the one where the woman was not raped or the man was not almost beaten to death or branded or his finger cut off or his ear cut off from trying to run away."[9]

But he has yet to get there.

Slavery was not just an institution. Neither is racism nor White supremacy. They are inadequate symbols of the savage, brutal struggle human beings created in God's image bravely faced each day, and they represent the nightmarish backdrop to every single deliberation of the church about slavery and racism.

Finally, a personal and pastoral word to the reader. This book grew from my work as a pastor at University UMC in Austin, Texas, a historically liberal congregation. I've written it as a handbook for pastors and laity. Not everyone who picks up this study will be at the same point in their journey to understand the meaning of racial justice in our time. We twenty-first-century Methodists are all over the map on racism—which is also true of our history. I've already made it clear that I believe racism goes beyond personal prejudices, and I acknowledge systemic racism and the many ways our institutions have been shaped by and for the preservation of White supremacy. This may not be where you are. You may not agree with some of what I've written for all kinds of reasons. You may feel like you've come to take swimming lessons, and the instructor is in the deep end of the pool inviting you to jump in.

---

9. Smith, *How the Word*, 76.

You may also struggle with this book because it invites you to grapple with a history quite different from what you might have learned about the Methodist Church since childhood. You may find yourself surprised or even shocked at how pastors and leaders, and even regular church members have behaved regarding race. You may need to take some time along the way to pause and reflect. I hope you know that these kinds of reactions are natural, and that the level of our discomfort in hearing these stories is rarely, if ever, a measure of the truth of these stories. If I've learned anything over the last decade, it is this: there is a direct relationship between the discomfort I'm willing to live with and own and how far down the road of understanding racism I can travel. I'd even go so far as to say that sacred discomfort can be a means of grace!

Wherever you are in the journey of understanding racism, White privilege, and White supremacy, I hope you approach what I've written with an open mind and heart. I hope you reflect deeply on our history, on the stories, and on the lives I've included here. I hope you dig into our past along with companions in your church and see how that past is still with us in the twenty-first century.

As we seek the truth together, may we also be inspired to work tirelessly for justice and for what historian Jemar Tisby calls "a more courageous Christianity."[10] If United Methodists are all about making disciples for the transformation of the world, I can think of no more transformative work than dismantling racism. If United Methodists are about to create a new church following a projected division in the near future, I can think of nothing more important or urgent!

Questions for Discussion

1. What early experiences made you aware of racism? What prompted you to act on them?

2. How do you react to the systemic definition of racism? How is systemic racism different from interpersonal personal racism?

3. Why is it important to learn the history of our United Methodist Church in regard to race? How might exploring our past have a role in shaping our future as a church?

10. Tisby, *Color of Compromise*, 24.

2

John Wesley and the Institution of Slavery

ISABELLE WILKERSON BEGINS HER remarkable book *Caste: The Origins of Our Discontents* with a striking image. She recalls a famous photograph from the Nazi era, a picture of shipyard workers in Hamburg, Germany, in 1936. All the workers raise their arms in the familiar salute to the Führer. Except one. In the upper right-hand corner, one man stands with his arms folded across his chest while everyone around him is saluting. "Looking back," Wilkerson notes, ". . . he is the only person in the entire scene who is on the right side of history."[1]

We now believe the man's name was August Landmesser. Even though the Nazi party had only been in power a few years, Landmesser had seen enough of the lies, the terror, and the disruption. We would like to think that, were we to find ourselves in a similar situation, we would have joined Landmesser. Surely we would have seen through Hitler and joined the resistance. We would never have raised our hands in salute.

But would we? To stand firm against the tide in any era requires enormous courage and resolve. Would we be willing to face the derision, scorn, and exclusion, perhaps even violence that would attend standing against profound injustice?

To make this question more specific to our subject, if we had lived in America in the late-eighteenth century, would we have risen up against slavery and joined the abolitionists? This is certainly one of the unresolved

---

1. Wilkerson, *Origins*, xv.

paradoxes of early Methodism. How did a movement that began with the antislavery sentiments of its founder, John Wesley, become so utterly complacent to the horrors of slavery? Much of the rest of this book is an attempt to unpack this unholy paradox.

Early Impressions

So what were Wesley's views on race, slavery, and the transatlantic enslaved trade? In this chapter, we'll unpack Wesley's antislavery journey, explore his tract "Thoughts upon Slavery," and reflect on the relationship between Wesley's theology and his views on slavery. We'll also take a look at two contemporaries of Wesley, John Newton and George Whitefield.

While it's quite possible that John Wesley came into contact with enslaved people in England, we know that both John and his brother Charles witnessed firsthand the brutal horrors of chattel slavery[2] during their sojourn in the colonies in the late 1730s. They were stationed in the Georgia colony, where there was an enforced ban on slavery, although it was legal in nearby South Carolina.

Following a visit to Charleston in 1736, Charles graphically reported the tyrannical practices of enslavers he observed, including driving nails through their ears and whipping and maiming the enslaved. In one case, he referred to an enslaver who battered a young enslaved woman nearly to death and poured hot wax on her. Her crime was overfilling a teacup.[3]

Charles concluded his account with the nightmarish absurdity of the legal system: "These horrid cruelties are the less to be wondered at, because the government itself, in effect, countenances and allows them to kill their slaves, by the ridiculous penalty appointed for it, of about seven pounds sterling, half of which is usually saved by the criminal's informing against himself. This I can look upon as no other than a public act to indemnify murder."[4]

Slavery clearly remained on John Wesley's mind. In his contact with those who were enslaved, Wesley showed an unusual amount of care. In 1758, Wesley reported in his journal that he baptized two Black converts

2. Chattel slavery is "the enslaving and owning of human beings and their offspring as common property, able to be bought, sold, and forced to work without wages." "Chattel Slavery," dictionary.com.

3. Smith, *John Wesley and Slavery*, 42.

4. Quoted in Smith, *John Wesley and Slavery*, 42.

and received them into the movement. In his accounts of conversations with enslaved persons, it's clear he thought they were spiritual beings in need of hearing the gospel. This may seem obvious to us, but at that time, the majority of folks, even in the church, questioned the full humanity of enslaved persons.[5]

Over the next three decades, references to enslavers ("man-stealers, the worst of all thieves") are scattered throughout his writings. He wrote that England's continuing engagement in the transatlantic slave trade was a national disgrace.[6] When Methodist societies were formed, Wesley prohibited enslavers from being members.

Wesley also joined in a familiar argument at the time that lampooned the hypocrisy of American independence. Some advocates of independence argued that Americans were enslaved persons because they didn't have political representation in parliament. Here is Wesley's counterargument:

> Slavery is a state wherein neither a man's goods, nor liberty, nor life, are at his own disposal. Such is that state of a thousand, of ten thousand, Negroes in the American colonies. And are their masters in the same state with them? . . . Have they no more disposal of their own goods, or livery, or lives? Does anyone beat or imprison them at pleasure; or take away their wives, or children, or lives; or sell them like cows or horses? This is slavery; and will you face us down that the Americans are in such slavery as this?[7]

Unfortunately for Wesley, his case for the pretense of American pleas for liberty became part of his overall opposition to American independence. Wesley was not supportive of American calls for independence, which created a few problems for Methodists during the Revolutionary War. No less than Francis Asbury said that Wesley's political views made him "the most obnoxious man in the new world."[8]

"Thoughts upon Slavery"

In 1772, Wesley wrote in his journal that he had been reading a book "published by an honest Quaker, on that execrable sum of all villainies, commonly called the Slave-trade." The book was written by Anthony Benezet, a

5. Brendlinger, *Social Justice*, 68.
6. Brendlinger, "John Wesley and Slavery," 226–27.
7. Wesley, "Thoughts upon Slavery," 109.
8. Morris-Chapman, "Methodist Responses," 40.

Philadelphia Quaker, whose early antislavery writings were a huge inspiration to other abolitionists, including John Wesley.[9]

Two years later, Wesley decided to enter the debate with the publishing of his tract "Thoughts upon Slavery." It's a modest piece, really a long pamphlet of just over fifty pages. Although Wesley made extensive use of the work of others, even opening himself to charges of plagiarism, the core of the work is his clear argument that slavery is completely immoral and entirely unjust.

One unexpected twist in Wesley's tract is that his arguments against slavery are not based on Scripture but on reason and natural law. Most of the proslavery writers made profuse use of biblical texts. We'll take time in chapter 3 to look more closely at how Methodists used Scripture to justify slavery. Here we can only speculate why Wesley chose this unusual methodology. Some think that Wesley may have understood Scripture and Christian faith as so opposed to slavery that making the case in his tract was unnecessary. It seems more likely to me that he was concerned that his tract gain a larger audience, knowing that some would not be persuaded by scriptural arguments alone or even at all.[10]

Looking at how the tract was received, this approach appears to have worked. It was distributed not only among Methodists but to persons of prominence, like Dr. Benjamin Rush, America's first Surgeon General. Over the next eight to ten years, it was one of the most widely read books on slavery in Britain and the colonies. It was so influential in the colonies that thirteen editions were printed over thirty years. One copy even found its way into George Washington's library.[11]

We'll spend most of the remainder of this chapter looking closely at Wesley's tract not only because of its key influence on the burgeoning antislavery movement, but also because it lays out much of the territory the church would cover as it struggled with slavery and racism in the century that followed. I'll begin by highlighting a number of the key arguments that Wesley makes.

1. Wesley begins the tract with an idealized description of Africa before the degradations of the slave trade, borrowed from a variety of contemporary sources. He's attacking the common myth that enslavers were

9. Smith, *John Wesley and Slavery*, 78.
10. See Field, "Public Theologian," for this argument.
11. Brendlinger, *Social Justice*, 24.

providing enslaved Africans a better life. On the contrary, Wesley says, African societies were characterized by peace, prosperity, and reverence for God, and that the people are cultured, friendly, and rational.

Early on, Wesley asks, where among the nations might one find the practice of "mercy, justice and truth?" One would expect the answer to be in Britain or Europe, but it was not so. If one seeks genuine honesty, one will find it in "Benin, Congo or Angola." One of the first well-known White religious leaders to challenge the stereotypes of Black persons, Wesley declared that they are "so far from being the stupid, senseless, brutish, lazy barbarians, the fierce, cruel, perfidious savages they have been described."[12] He calls out the mythology of the superiority of European culture and people that was pervasive in his time with a simple rejoinder: all of us "have the same flesh and blood."

Historian Irv Brendliger, in his book on John Wesley's social thought, sums up Wesley on racial equality: "Wesley stood for and practiced an egalitarianism that would not be lived up to by many in succeeding generations, even those in the tradition he began."[13]

2. Wesley was most concerned with developing his argument that the institution of slavery was inconsistent with the trinity of "justice, mercy and truth." He provides a litany of the violence of slavery and the enslaved trade so utterly out of sync with any sensible notions of mercy that it hardly even requires proof. At one point, he cries out, "Did the Creator intend that the noblest creature in the whole world should live such a life as this? 'Are these thy glorious works, Parent of Good?'"[14]

Given the abject horrors of every aspect of slavery, Wesley goes almost as far as to justify slave rebellions: they are "asserting their natural liberty, which they have as much right to as the air they breathe." In words that seem decidedly un-Wesleyan, he asks enslavers: "What wonder if they should cut your throat? And if they did, whom could you thank for it but yourself? You first acted the villain in making them enslaved persons whether you stole them or bought them."[15]

3. Slavery is also inconsistent with justice. For Wesley, all humans are endowed with liberty as a natural right, and one cannot deprive another

12. Wesley, "Thoughts," 64.
13. Brendlinger, *Social Justice*, 71.
14. Wesley, "Thoughts," 68.
15. Wesley, "Thoughts," 75.

of those natural rights: "Liberty is the right of every human creature, as soon as he breathes the vital air."[16] It's worth quoting Wesley at length here to observe the passion with which he makes his case:

> Where is the justice of inflicting the severest evils, on those who have done us no wrong? Of depriving those that never injured us in word or deed, of every comfort of life? Of tearing them from their native country, and depriving them of liberty itself. . . . Yea where is the justice of taking away the lives of innocent, inoffensive men? Murdering thousands of them in their own land, by the hands of their own countrymen: Many thousands, year after year, on shipboard, and then casting them like dung into the sea! And tens of thousands in that cruel slavery, to which they are so unjustly reduced? But waving, for the present, all other considerations, I strike at the root of this complicated villainy. I absolutely deny all slave-holding to be consistent with any degree of even natural justice.[17]

Oddly enough, the injustice of slavery was often defended as legal simply because state law authorized it. But Wesley quickly put that weak argument to rest: "The grand plea is, 'They are authorized by law.' But can law, human law, change the nature of things? Can it turn darkness into light, or evil into good? By no means. . . . So that I still ask, Who can reconcile this treatment of the Negroes, first and last, with either mercy or justice?"[18]

4. One of the most common arguments offered by enslavers was that slavery was an absolute necessity. Should it be abolished, they said, the country would collapse into poverty and economic ruin. John Wesley made quick work of this argument. There could never be an occasion where one would have to violate the natural laws of justice, mercy, and truth. "No circumstances can make it necessary for a man to burst in sunder all the ties of humanity."[19]

Some pressed this argument further, saying that slavery was necessary because Africans were more suited to working in the hot climate of the South. This sounds absolutely preposterous to the modern

16. Wesley, "Thoughts," 73.
17. Wesley, "Thoughts," 70.
18. Wesley, "Thoughts," 70.
19. Wesley, "Thoughts," 72.

ear, but this was part of the structure supporting slavery, which Wesley was undoing. Even so eminent a contemporary as George Whitfield argued along these lines. "Georgia," he wrote, "never can or will be a flourishing province without negroes."[20]

Wesley related his own experience in Georgia to dismiss this rationalization of enslavement: "I and my family (eight in number) did employ all our spare time there, in felling of trees and clearing of ground, as hard labour as any Negro need be employed in. . . . And this was so far from impairing our health, that we all continued perfectly well, while the idle ones round about us were swept away as with a pestilence."[21]

John Wesley's understanding of the use of money also came into play when he tackled the argument that slavery was justified on economic grounds. At first glance, one might imagine that enslavers could argue that they're just following Wesley. They're simply gaining all they can by using all their available resources. They might recite Wesley's oft-quoted slogan, "gain all you can, save all you can, give all you can."[22]

However, a closer reading of his sermon "The Use of Money," from which this three-part saying is plucked, clarifies that for Wesley, there are many ways to gain money that are strictly out of bounds for the faithful. Wesley's advice is that one gains all one can without harming oneself or one's neighbor, which obviously ruled out slavery. At one point in his antislavery tract he agrees that using enslaved people could well gain one great riches, and then adds, "But how is this necessary? It is very possible you might be both a better and a happier man, if you had not a quarter of it. I deny that your gaining one thousand enslaved persons is necessary either to your present or eternal happiness."[23] By the same token, neither is the labor of the enslaved necessary to the economy's overall health. "Better no trade," he writes, "than trade procured by villainy."[24]

20. Quoted in Brendlinger, *Social Justice*, 52.
21. Wesley, "Thoughts," 73.
22. See Outler, *John Wesley*, 238–50, for Wesley's sermon, "The Use of Money."
23. Wesley, "Thoughts, 39.
24. Wesley, "Thoughts," 74.

5. Finally, we consider how Wesley handled those who argued that enslaved persons had to be treated so treacherously to get them to work. He flipped the argument on its head, declaring that what enslavers saw as inferiority in those they enslaved was not the *reason* for slavery but the direct *result* of slavery. Historian Irv Brendliger calls this "the cycle of degradation."[25] Slavery degrades the lived existence of the enslaved and also the lives of the enslavers.

What Wesley is grappling with here is the notion that slavery as a system has had and would continue to have a long-lasting and damaging impact on Black persons and White enslavers. The blame for creating this vast system of inequalities falls squarely on the enslavers, on White people. In his words, "you first acted the villain in making them enslaved persons (whether you sold them or bought them). You kept them stupid and wicked by cutting them off from all opportunities of improving either in knowledge or in virtue."[26] For there to be healing and transformation for the enslaved and enslavers, slavery must be abolished.

It's worth noting again that Wesley's little tract is not simply a dispassionate analysis of slavery. The language is often fiery and highly personal, designed not simply to move the mind but to convert the heart. Here's a sample of the level of enthusiastic feeling Wesley marshaled to convict traders. Wesley begins with simple questions about their humanity: "Are you *a man*? Then you should have [a] *human* heart. But have you indeed? What is your heart made of? Is there no such principle as compassion there? . . . When you saw the flowing eyes, the heaving breasts, the bleeding sides and tortured limbs of your fellow-creatures, [were] you a stone, or a brute?"

And then Wesley drops the hammer. If, after considering the pain and anguish of those they enslaved, they are still not moved to yield to God's mercy and change their ways, "then will the great GOD deal with *you*, as you have dealt with *them*, and require all their blood at your hands. And at that day it shall be more tolerable for *Sodom* and *Gomorrah* than for you!"[27]

In January 1788, Wesley preached in Bristol in the New Room, the oldest Methodist Meeting House in England. That same year, the

25. Brendlinger, *Social Justice*, 54.
26. Wesley, "Thoughts," 75.
27. Wesley, "Thoughts," 77.

abolition of slavery was on everyone's mind; it was the beginning of a national campaign to petition for the end of the enslaved trade. Bristol's economy depended heavily on the enslaved trade. Wesley's topic for the evening service? The abolition of slavery.

A remarkable event interrupted the evening service that Wesley described vividly in his journal:

> About the middle of the discourse . . . a vehement noise arose, none could tell why, and shot like lightening through the whole congregation The terror and confusion were inexpressible. You might have imagined it was a city taken by storm. The people rushed up on each other with the utmost violence; the benches were broke in pieces; and nine-tenths of the congregation appeared to be struck with the same panic. In about six minutes the storm ceased, almost as suddenly as it rose; and, all being calm, I went on without the least interruption.[28]

If Wesley's rhetoric approached the inflammatory level of his address to the traders quoted above, it is no wonder that a huge commotion erupted in the church. Even more surprising that Wesley was able to finish his sermon!

A Witness to the End

Wesley's witness against slavery continued to the end of his days. The abolition of slavery emerged as one of the dominant themes. At the age of ninety in a letter to his friend, Henry Moore, Wesley wrote: "I would do anything that is in my power toward the extirpation of that trade which is a scandal not only to Christianity, but humanity."[29]

The last book Wesley recorded reading was *The Interesting Narrative of the Life of Olaudah Equiano, or Gustavus Vassa, the African,* one of the first widely-read narratives of an enslaved person. Equiano was born in Africa in 1745, taken by hunters, and sold as an enslaved person in Barbados. He was ultimately freed and served for a time in the British navy. Wesley was particularly struck by the colonial law that a Black person wronged by a

---

28. Quoted in Smith, *John Wesley and Slavery,* 74–75. See also Carey, "Language of the Heart," 277.

29. Quoted in Brendlinger, *Social Justice,* 39.

White person had no redress: "it being a law in all our Colonies that the oath of a black against a white goes for nothing. What villainy is this!"[30]

In his narrative, Equiano offers this challenge to Christians on the horrors of the enslaved trade: "O, ye nominal Christians! Might not an African ask you, learned you this from your God, who says unto you, Do unto all men as you would men should do unto you?"[31] The hypocrisy of Christians in supporting chattel slavery was not lost on many who were enslaved. I like to imagine that Wesley underlined this passage in his copy and wrote "YES!" in the margins.

Within the week before his death, Wesley wrote his final letter to William Wilberforce, the member of British parliament who emerged as the leader of the abolition of the enslaved trade. The letter is one of encouragement in the heavy opposition Wilberforce faced and prayers for God's blessing: "O be not weary of well doing! Go on, in the name of God and in the power of His might, till even American slavery (the vilest that ever saw the sun) shall vanish away before it."[32]

Slavery and Methodist Principles

John Wesley's strong antislavery response throughout his life is not unexpected, given some of the basic principles of his theology. Wesley's teaching that salvation was open to all stood in sharp contrast to the hyper-Calvinism of the eighteenth century that reserved salvation for the select few. Methodist teachings were much more egalitarian, allowing for the possibility of change and transformation by the inner working of God's Spirit (sanctification). Calvinism led in a different direction, that one's place in the divinely ordered world was set and not to be disturbed.

Historian Peter Murray talks about the centrality of the change of heart experience to Wesley. By God's grace, one received a new identity in Christ that freed a person from all other claims. "This new status . . . freed persons of 'normal' expectations, conditions, and rituals." It shattered the old life and opened up a new life of new possibilities for everyone.[33]

Wesley's rejection of the idea that one's position in the world was set by God and could never be changed surely brought a measure of hope to his

30. Phipps, "John Wesley on Slavery," 28–29.

31. Equiano, *Interesting Narrative*, 26.

32. Outler, *John Wesley*, 85–86.

33. Murray, *Crucible of Race*, 10.

followers. It conveyed a sense of responsibility that one could take charge of one's situation in life. One's plight in life as an enslaved person, for example, was not a permanent condition ordained by God. As one can imagine, this teaching was embraced by many enslaved and outcast persons.

Wesley's view also meant that more significant social problems were not beyond repair. For many in the eighteenth century, the institution of slavery was considered part of God's sovereign purposes for humanity in a fallen world. Wesley's theology of grace and salvation for all challenged this. Slavery was not a permanent feature of the landscape; it could not only be challenged but eventually abolished, a view that gained significant influence by the end of the century.

Finally, Wesley's understanding of human transformation by the Spirit of God was not limited to the inner life. By definition, the renewal of the heart gave way to work on behalf of one's neighbor. Perhaps the most famous Wesley quote on this topic is this: "Holy Solitaries is a phrase no more consistent with the gospel than Holy Adulterers. The gospel of Christ knows of no religion, but social; no holiness but social holiness. Faith working by love, is the length and breadth and depth and height of Christian perfection."[34] For Wesley, there was no such thing as faith focused on personal piety; it was a contradiction in terms. Solitary religion disconnected from works of mercy and justice was simply not a possibility for Wesleyans.

While Wesley believed that slavery as a social evil had to be addressed, he seemed reluctant to offer a social solution. Of course, Wesley lived long before the emergence of ideas about systemic and structural evil and that institutions are arranged in ways that privilege certain people at the cost of impoverishing and oppressing others.[35] Wesley worked on the premise that converted persons would be like leaven, transforming and improving society on all levels. His hope for an end to slavery lay initially with changing individuals directly involved in trading human beings. Reformed hearts would end slavery.[36]

Toward the end of his life, though, Wesley seemed more aware of the power of the institution of slavery and that hope for social change must be directed at laws that maintained the institution. In an early antislavery trade campaign in 1787, he urged his followers in Manchester to petition parliament, which they did in great numbers. He also distributed his "Thoughts

34. Wesley, *Hymns and Sacred Poems*, viii.
35. Moe-Lobeda, *Resisting*, 12.
36. Brendlinger, *Social Justice*, 129–46.

upon Slavery" throughout England. Methodists continued to play a crucial role in that petition and in future campaigns to end the enslaved trade and ultimately emancipate all those enslaved in England.[37]

Two Contemporaries of John Wesley

Before diving into the post-Wesley period in America, I'll highlight two key individuals who were contemporaries of John Wesley and were deeply influenced by the Methodist movement—John Newton and George Whitefield.

1. Even though John Newton was not, strictly speaking, a Methodist, we need to include him not only because of his connections with John Wesley but because of his composition of a perennial favorite Methodist hymn, "Amazing Grace." The oft-told but erroneous story is that John Newton was a converted English captain of enslaving ships, and that this hymn was written as a testimony to God's grace calling him out of the ghastly cruelty of that trade into a new life. Oddly enough, Newton's conversion actually led him into the trade. He called it his "respectable vocation." Newton, like so many others in the church of his time, saw no contradiction between his new faith and slavery until much later in life.[38]

   Newton did leave the enslaved trade in 1754, not because of a moral conversion, but because of health problems, although he continued to invest in the trade. Eventually, he expressed his opposition to the trade in humans, but never to slavery. This was a crucial difference between Newton and John Wesley and the abolitionists who followed him, who understood that it was not enough to shut down the trade in human lives or fix the abuses. Chattel slavery must be uprooted and ended because the entire system was rotten to the core. Newton may be better remembered as a spiritual counselor to William Wilberforce, assuring him that he could serve God in Parliament, where he later became one of England's foremost abolitionists.

2. George Whitefield, an Anglican minister, was something of a prodigy. Following his conversion in 1735 at the age of twenty-one, he was already preaching revivals up and down the colonial coast and on both sides of the Atlantic. Whitefield became the leading star in what

---

37. Brendlinger, *Social Justice*, 165–70.
38. Brendlinger, "John Wesley and Slavery," 231.

would later be called the First Great Awakening, a period of revival that was transforming religion in America. In the words of sociologists Rodney Finke and Rodney Stark, George Whitefield was "quite simply one of the most powerful and moving preachers ever to hold forth." One contemporary observed that Whitefield "could move men to tears or make them tremble by his simple intonations in pronouncing the word Mesopotamia."[39]

Whitefield was an early supporter of the Methodist movement. He attended Oxford and was one of the founding members of the Holy Club with John and Charles Wesley. Whitefield was a primary influence in encouraging Wesley to "be more vile" and preach outdoors, which Wesley did on numerous occasions to large crowds. (Wesley confessed to being quite tenacious about decency and order in a worship service.) Theological differences, however, over predestination and a desire to focus on his evangelistic work led Whitefield to break with Wesley, although they remained friends and colleagues to the end. In fact, Wesley preached at Whitefield's funeral in 1770.[40]

In spite of his extraordinary eloquence, Whitefield was a man of contradictions, especially when it came to slavery. Early on, he railed in sermons against enslavers. But after establishing an orphanage in Georgia, he actually argued for the introduction of enslaved humans into Georgia. In 1751, he wrote a letter to Wesley laying out his plans, using all the usual arguments. The enslaved were needed for the orphanage to survive. The work there would be a boon to them, perhaps even an opportunity for their conversion. When slavery became legal in Georgia, he procured fifty enslaved people for work at the Bethesda orphanage who were, in his words, "brought in a wrong way from their own country" but what could one do about it? Besides, he could "make their lives comfortable."[41]

Whitefield displayed some of the deep contradictions about slavery that would bedevil the church for decades to come. He believed that those enslaved were "by nature, no worse nor no better than Whites."[42] But he was also an enslaver and was at peace with slavery. He treated the enslaved as human beings capable of receiving and

---

39. Both quotes are from Emerson and Smith, *Divided by Faith*, 25.
40. Brendlinger, *Social Justice*, 3–6.
41. Brendlinger, *Social Justice*, 57–58.
42. Quoted in Painter, "Pro-Slavery Argument," 34.

responding to the gospel. Yet he was instrumental in extending a system into Georgia that treated the enslaved as property. He stood against the abuses of slavery but was somehow not opposed to the institution of slavery.

In this early period, Whitefield was something of an outlier. Most early Methodist leaders—Wesley, Asbury, Coke—were committed to ending slavery. Unfortunately, the future direction of the Methodist Church would more closely follow the compromised views of George Whitefield than those of John Wesley.

Conclusion

Wesley's view of slavery was a marvelous foundation for those first American Methodists, but it was not without flaws. He was very slow to urge his followers to take their case to the governing powers to end slavery. As strong as his condemnation of slavery was, he never proposed a plan for how it might end.

Wesley also failed to connect his arguments against slavery with Scripture or theology. In the next chapter, we'll find that Methodists who tolerated slavery were quick to ground their arguments in texts from the Bible, while abolitionists struggled with texts to bolster their views.

Finally, much of Wesley's writing against slavery proposed ending it by transforming the hearts of those responsible for enslaving others. This personal approach to a decidedly social problem will confound Methodists as they face the challenges of slavery, racism, and segregation in the nineteenth century and beyond.

Even so, Wesley accomplished a world of good in his lifetime. He passed on to his followers a powerful antislavery sentiment and a series of solid moral arguments that effectively undid much of the intellectual underpinning of the institution of slavery and racism. He is a model for his followers of how to use one's voice and privilege on behalf of those who are marginalized and oppressed. Regrettably, that model would prove hard to emulate when faced directly with the burgeoning juggernaut of American chattel slavery.

Questions for Discussion

1. Were you surprised by Wesley's outspokenness against slavery, given that Great Britain had a lucrative slave trade? Do you see any problems with his view?

2. What arguments in support of slavery did he refute in his pamphlet "Thoughts upon Slavery"?

3. How did his theological perspective on human nature influence his views on slavery?

4. Based on his arguments against slavery, how do you think Wesley would critique our present-day economic system?

3

Methodists Struggle with Slavery

ALEXIS DE TOCQUEVILLE, A French aristocrat and philosopher, made some unusually prescient observations about the United States in his classic work *Democracy in America*. In 1835 Tocqueville foresaw that the issue of racial inequality in our country would be a long and difficult struggle. He wrote: "I do not imagine the white and black races will ever live in any country upon an equal footing," and he believed this would be especially so in the United States.[1]

Just as the nation struggled with the paradox of enslaved peoples in a free land, so did the church. John Wesley could not have made it any clearer that slavery was not only inconsistent with any notion of justice but also that fierce opposition to it was the only position possible for those who trusted in the grace of God offered to all. Yet, in the decades following Wesley, the Methodist Church would find itself so entangled with the institutions of slavery and racism that it often functioned not so much as a transformer but as a transmitter of the evils of slavery and White supremacy.

In this chapter, we'll explore the various ways Methodists approached the horror of slavery and the lives of the enslaved. Eventually their irreconcilable views led to a break in the church between northern and southern Methodism. We'll approach this history by engaging the way the larger church moved quickly toward complicity with racism and slavery and considering some of the key personalities on both sides of the debate.

1. Tocqueville, *Democracy*, 411.

The Methodist Church Responds to Slavery

The Methodist movement began with a solid antislavery platform. Methodist societies had been formed in America before the Revolution, and enslavers and those engaged in the enslaved trade were not allowed to be members. Francis Asbury, who became the first bishop in the newly formed Methodist Episcopal Church (MEC), declared early on that Methodists must follow the Quakers in calling for the liberation of those enslaved or they would surely suffer God's displeasure. In the winter of 1778, Asbury wrote, "I have lately been impressed with a deep concern, for bringing about the freedom of slaves in America, and feel resolved to do what I can to promote it."[2] Harry Hosier, one of Methodism's first Black preachers, often traveled with Asbury and Coke on preaching tours.

However, an early conference in 1780 reflected an underlying ambivalence toward enslaved Black Methodists. While passing strong antislavery language, they also urged a disturbing paternalism, requiring White supervision and a curfew for gatherings of Black Methodists.[3] "White Methodists recognized that slavery was wrong, but had great difficulty in seeing the way through to genuine equality and to the importance of embracing Black leadership to develop."[4]

Sent by Wesley to help organize the new church in America, Thomas Coke helped craft a strong statement opposing slavery. In the last week of 1784, the founding conference of the MEC, often called the Christmas conference, was held. Conference organizers adopted Coke's strict stance against slavery. All Methodists, both lay members and preachers, were required to free those they had enslaved. The buying and selling of enslaved persons was absolutely prohibited. And those who did not emancipate their enslaved persons would be expelled from the church.[5]

The new rule, which expanded on the church's General Rules, was not received well, and as a consequence, both Coke and Asbury had to deal with a surprising level of hostility and opposition. In 1785, preaching in a barn in Virginia, Coke was threatened by a mob. One witness reported that

2. Richey et al., *Methodist Experience*, 1:14. All quotations are from the second edition unless otherwise indicated.

3. Richey et al., *Methodist Experience*, 1:18.

4. Richey et al., *Methodist Experience*, 1:18.

5. The General Rules of the MEC listed "the buying and selling of men, women, or children, with an intention to enslave them" as one of the particular sins that Methodists should avoid. See Mathews, *Slavery and Methodism*, 9.

a fashionably dressed woman went out and offered fifty rioters a large reward if the mob would administer one hundred lashes to Dr. Coke. Thankfully, Coke managed to escape without incident.[6] However, because of that opposition, and in the interests of evangelizing the enslaved, Coke began to water down his message so as not to upset enslavers.[7]

The new rules about slavery were so unpopular that, at the next conference just a half year later, the fledgling Methodist Church suspended them, and the church began a rapid slide into compromise and complicity with slavery. Even Asbury himself, who spoke so strongly against slavery, found it hard to stand consistently against it. During the Revolutionary War, he had hidden in the home of an enslaver and was cared for by enslaved persons. He was also known to be a frequent guest of one of the largest enslavers in Maryland.[8] While both Coke and Asbury were strongly opposed to slavery, for practical reasons each one chose to muffle their opposition for the sake of unity and church growth.[9]

There were several reasons behind the fierce pushback against the new rules about slavery. First, southern Methodists, like other landowners, assumed their prosperity would be built on the backs of enslaved human beings. And southerners were also a majority in the early Methodist Church. As the cotton kingdom grew, so did the perceived need for more and more enslaved humans. Growing cotton without enslaved labor was considered economically unfeasible.

Second, the growing Methodist movement was rooted in revivals, and many thought that antislavery rhetoric would hurt the church's growth, especially in the South. The subsequent startling growth of the church in the early nineteenth century was, oddly enough, seen as confirmation by some that God had rewarded them because they had made the right decision in watering down the rules to abolish slavery.

A third reason, connected to the second, was the strong evangelical commitment to preach the gospel to all, including those who were enslaved. In order to have access to enslaved persons, Methodist preachers softened the antislavery message so as not to alienate enslavers.[10] Few early Method-

---

6. Richard M. Cameron, "New Church Takes Root," in Bucke et al., *American Methodism*, 1:254.

7. Brendlinger, "John Wesley and Slavery," 235.

8. Straker, "Embracing the Whole Truth."

9. Brendlinger, "John Wesley and Slavery," 237.

10. See Mathews, *Slavery and Methodism*, 22–25 for development of these reasons.

ists were willing to face the elephant in the room—that preaching a gospel of liberation to a people enslaved was a complete contradiction. Prosperity, personal piety, and church growth won the day over emancipation.

Methodists usually gathered together every four years in a General Conference, but little was said about slavery until 1796. There, sweeping moral statements were made, like this: "we are more than ever convinced of the great evil of . . . slavery which still exists in these United States."[11] And yet little practical action was recommended beyond excluding members who actually bought or sold enslaved persons. Antislavery laws continued to be fiercely debated by conferencing Methodists; however, the call to action by preachers opposed to slavery seemed to have little effect on the general direction of the church. The church seemed unwilling and unable to confront the great evils of this system and hold their own membership accountable.

In 1800, in Charleston, South Carolina, two courageous Methodist preachers, George Dougherty and John Harper, decided to publish and distribute leaflets that were part of a campaign to encourage the gradual emancipation of those enslaved in states where emancipation was legal. So intense were the feelings at this time that a mob in Charleston burned the leaflets and then turned on one of the preachers, George Dougherty. They dragged him through the streets to a water pump, planning to drown him. One of his members thrust her shawl into the pump spout to slow down the flow of water just as a man approached the mob with a drawn sword to rescue the preacher![12]

Asbury, discouraged and resigned to the compromise the church had made with slavery, lamented that "there [was] not a sufficient sense of religion nor of liberty to destroy it; Methodists, Baptists, Presbyterians, in the highest flight of rapturous piety, still maintain and defend it."[13] Even so, Asbury and several Methodist leaders persisted, asking GC1800 to petition state governments to pass legislation that would codify gradual emancipation. The Conference did not take up their efforts.

Given the combative climate, Methodists continued to dilute rules for freeing those who were enslaved. The official rules and regulations for the MEC are captured in a book published every four years called the *Book of Discipline*. A particularly low point was reached in 1804 when the

11. Richard M. Cameron, "New Church Takes Root," in Bucke et al., *American Methodism*, 1:256.

12. The story is recounted in Mathews, *Slavery and Methodism*, 21–22.

13. Quoted in Mathews, *Slavery and Methodism*, 23.

whole section on slavery was omitted from the *Discipline* for Methodists south of Virginia. Now two copies of the *Discipline* circulated in the church—one for the antislavery North and the other for the proslavery South. In 1808, the MEC treaded further into compromise, deciding that the rules about the buying and selling of Black people could now be decided by annual conferences.[14]

The division of the church had begun in earnest. With growing opposition even to conversations about slavery, denunciation of it became increasingly difficult. In 1818 presiding elder Jacob Gruber preached a three-point sermon at a camp meeting in Maryland. His third point was the sin of slavery. He argued that it was not only against the Declaration of Independence, it was dangerous. It could lead to the murder of enslavers, a questionable argument that completely dodged concern for the constant danger the enslaved faced!

Imagining that Gruber was inciting an insurrection, he was indicted by a grand jury for disturbing "the tranquility, good order and government of the State of Maryland." Gruber was ultimately found not guilty and was advised to be more careful in his use of language to convict his audience of sin. It seems, though, that the warning missed its target, as Gruber later quipped "I have heard of Republican slaveholders, but I understand no more what it means than sober drunkards."[15]

The African Methodist Episcopal Church

Unequal treatment and outright racism in the church ultimately led Richard Allen to help found the African Methodist Episcopal Church (AME). Allen was born enslaved in Philadelphia. Following his introduction to Methodism as a teen, he soon converted and began preaching in various Methodist churches. On one occasion, Freeborn Garrettson visited the home of Allen's enslaver at Allen's invitation. Moved by Garrettson's preaching about renouncing slavery, his enslaver allowed Allen to work toward buying his freedom.[16]

---

14. The General Conference authorized each annual conference to "form [its] own regulations, relative to buying and selling slaves." Mathews, *Slavery and Methodism*, 26.

15. Republicans were opposed to slavery, so "Republican slaveholders" should be a non sequitur. Mathews, *Slavery and Methodism*, 36–37.

16. Dickerson, *African Methodist Episcopal*, 27.

Allen was licensed to preach and finally bought his freedom in 1786. He was invited to become a regular preacher at St. George's in Philadelphia for the Black membership. The catch? His services were to be held at five a.m. so as not to interfere with services for Whites! In addition to this, other practices made it clear that Black worshipers in the church were not full members of the church: White pastors continued to lead Black congregations, Black candidates for ministry were not being ordained as elders, and Black congregations had to pay fees for White pastors to administer the sacraments.[17] Historian Peter Murray wonders what the future of the church might have looked like had Methodist leadership been more open to Black pastors. Perhaps the church could have remained a biracial denomination.[18]

The last straw came in 1787[19] when Allen and his colleague Rev. Absalom Jones were asked to move from the section of St. George's reserved for Whites to a segregated area. Jones asked if the trustee might wait until after prayers were finished, but the trustee was insistent. Another trustee came over to help by physically pulling up Black worshipers who were kneeling for prayer.

Allen led them out of the church and said later, "We all went out of the church in a body, and they were no more plagued with us in the church."[20] Even under threat of expulsion from the MEC, Allen and his followers worshiped separately in a rented store room. In 1794 Bethel African Church was founded, and none other than Francis Asbury preached the inaugural sermon. Allen became the first Black deacon in the MEC when Asbury ordained him in 1799. White church leaders were unwilling to relinquish control of the church until, shockingly, in 1816, the Pennsylvania Supreme Court ruled in favor of the Black church's right to self-determination. Bethel Church grew to be one of the largest Methodist Churches in this period.[21]

In 1816, Richard Allen gathered Black leaders from several states to organize the AME Church, with Allen himself elected as the first bishop. This was one in a series of exoduses of Black Christians from White churches

17. Straker, "Non-Merging Streams," 96.

18. Murray, *Crucible of Race*, 15.

19. There is some question about the date of the walkout and exactly what transpired. Allen biographer Richard Newman suggests that Allen may have conceived a plan in 1787 that would galvanize both Black and White support for a new Black Church, a plan that he carried out in 1792 following the confrontation that he records in his autobiography. Those dates are the two prime candidates. See Newman, *Freedom's Prophet*, 63–68.

20. Quoted in Newman, *Freedom's Prophet*, 64.

21. Norwood, *American Methodism*, 168–71.

and was quite a blow to White paternalism. Similar discriminatory acts in New York led to the formation of the African Methodist Episcopal Zion Church (AMEZ) in 1821.

Methodist historian Frederick Norwood makes the crucial point that Allen's work went far beyond church organizing; his work can be understood as "an early expression of Black Power or Nationalism, since he engaged actively in projects for the economic and political betterment of black people, which included the boycott of slave-made goods."[22] Allen felt that African Methodism was the best chance for a renewal of Wesleyan Christianity, a strong opposition to slavery, and a renewed emphasis on egalitarianism.[23] In many ways, Richard Allen was a religious genius and the perfect embodiment of John Wesley in his time, especially in the way he combined vital piety with a powerful social witness.[24]

Colonization and the Mission to the Enslaved

By the 1830s, the church, like the nation, had splintered in several directions in response to slavery. In the North, abolitionists grew in strength and numbers. In response, Methodists in the South began to speak and write about slavery, attempting to justify it on biblical and moral grounds. We'll look in more detail at both of these groups below.

But first, we'll consider folks who tried to have it both ways—moderate Methodists in the North who were against slavery but who also saw abolitionists as agitators who were out to destroy the peace and prosperity of the church. Moderate Methodists tried to stake out a place in the middle by focusing on helping those who were enslaved in two ways: through the colonization movement and the mission to the enslaved humans.

1. The Society for the Colonization of Free People of Color of the United States was founded in 1816 by a Presbyterian minister, Robert Finley. The purpose of the organization was to send free African Americans to evangelize Africa. One motivation behind this movement was the sense that free Black persons in the United States would never be able

---

22. Norwood, *American Methodism*, 171.

23. Dickerson, *African Methodist Episcopal*, 34.

24. Black worshipers walked out in several cities—Baltimore, New York, and Charleston—over the increasing segregation of Black members.

to escape the demeaning impact of White supremacy and racism.[25] Colonization also drew supporters who simply feared growing numbers of freed Black people. And so it's a real question whether the colonizers themselves could escape the charge of racism, given their generally low opinion of Black persons.

Methodists didn't immediately jump on board with colonization efforts, especially when news came back of the disastrous first colonization expedition marred by death from tropical disease, mismanagement, and treachery. Methodist missionary zeal, however, soon prevailed, and Methodists quickly enlisted in the cause. It wasn't long before Methodist publications and annual conferences were awash with acclaim for the benefits of colonization.

The movement was not without its strong detractors. Abolitionist and editor William Lloyd Garrison harangued the proponents of colonization for perpetuating slavery and undercutting the work of elevating Black people in this country. Garrison also found advocates of colonization to be profoundly inconsistent. On the one hand, Garrison wrote, organizers declare that "free blacks are pests in the community." On the other hand, they propose that, if sent to Africa, formerly enslaved persons will become "the missionaries of salvation, who are to illumine all of Africa." Garrison deftly skewers this contradiction by declaring that "neither a sea voyage nor an African climate has any miraculous influence on the brain." If Black Americans can do well overseas, they would fare much better "among a civilized and christian [sic] people."[26]

In the final analysis, the movement to relocate Black Americans to what would become Liberia proved to be mostly smoke and mirrors. The expense, the horrendous mortality rates of those who were removed, and the sheer impracticality of the whole venture should have brought a quicker and more merciful end to the project. Ultimately, only a few thousand out of the millions of Black persons in the country emigrated. Historian Donald Mathews sums it up nicely: "Colonization was created to meet the needs of minds overwhelmed by a complex moral problem; it became a gentle, wistful hope of readjusting social dislocation painlessly."[27]

25. Morris-Chapman, "Methodist Responses," 44.
26. Garrison, *Thoughts*, 155–56.
27. Mathews, *Slavery and Methodism*, 110.

2. If Methodists could not free the enslaved on earth, they could surely free them for life in the hereafter. Preaching the gospel to those enslaved had long been a central mission of the Methodist Church, and, as antislavery voices swelled, it became the moral alternative to abolition and the best way to help those who were enslaved.

Black members were in the MEC from the beginning. For a brief period in the late eighteenth century, Black and White Christians met together in worship services and class meetings. But the dominant pattern soon became segregated classes and balconies for the enslaved. By 1790, one-fifth of the membership of the MEC was Black.

Part of the reason Black Americans responded so well to the Methodist Church was that, at least at its inception, it had taken a strong antislavery position and was willing to include Black members in its membership. Historian Peter Murray adds an additional reason: its orality. "[Methodism] was a religious movement rooted in preaching, praise, and hymn singing." Since enslaved Black members were limited in their access to literacy, they found power in oral communication.[28]

Ministry to enslaved persons began before the founding of the denomination, and it was not very popular with most enslavers. Many simply did not believe that those enslaved had souls and hence could not be saved. In the wake of several well-publicized revolts of the enslaved, there was also widespread concern that preaching might lead to insurrection and violence.

It seems that Methodist enthusiasm again prevailed and, despite the obstacles, the missions were fairly successful. The numbers, however, belie a host of problems with the mission. Historian Jemar Tisby observes that the missions were dominated by paternalistic attitudes where equality was spiritualized.[29] In other words, the inner freedom one experienced as a new Christian believer did not outwardly result in any change of status for enslaved Black Christians. Conversion did not equal emancipation.

One of the great hopes of the missioners to the enslaved was that the gospel would transform the hearts of enslavers in preparation for the emancipation of the enslaved. By the 1820s, it's difficult to imagine the effort this would have taken, given how tightly slavery's tentacles

28. Murray, *Crucible of Race*, 12.
29. Tisby, *Color of Compromise*, 66.

were wrapped around everything. And there is little evidence that many enslavers were in fact transformed by the gospel.

In 1845 Frederick Douglass wrote about his new enslaver, Thomas Auld, describing him as "well matched, being equally mean and cruel." Auld attended a Methodist camp meeting and claimed to have been converted. Douglass was initially optimistic that this would result in better treatment, perhaps even emancipation. In fact, Christian Auld returned worse. Douglass put it this way: "Prior to his conversion, he relied upon his own depravity to shield and sustain him in his savage barbarity; but after his conversion, he found religious sanction and support for his slaveholding cruelty."[30] Douglass made it clear that this was not unusual behavior among converted enslavers.

Here we see the church not only supporting slavery, but providing divine cover for its barbarity and violence. What is equally troubling is that with all of the missions going on, the MEC did nothing to humanize the treatment of the enslaved. Instead, there was a push to use the mission to improve the morality of the enslaved, which really meant assuring the enslaved were obedient and hard-working.

Anson West, in *A History of Methodism in Alabama*, recounts a bizarre interchange between a missionary and a person enslaved which illustrates how far the gospel had skidded off the tracks. "The missionary asked, What did God make you for? The slave answered, To make a crop. The missionary asked, What is the meaning of 'Thou shalt not commit adultery.' The slave answered, To serve our heavenly Father, our earthly master, our overseer, and not steal anything."[31]

Colonization and the mission to those enslaved functioned more to soothe the conscience of moderate Whites who were antislavery but somehow could not wrap their minds around abolition. Both also added fuel to the insidious notion that one could support the enslaved without doing anything to end slavery. This paradoxical thinking about race will raise its ugly head often in the decades that follow.

Methodist Abolitionists

Several events helped foster a strong resurgence of antislavery action in the 1830s, and Methodists played key roles. The primary motivator was

30. Quoted in Jones, *White Too Long*, 87.

31. Quoted in Mathews, *Slavery and Methodism*, 87.

William Lloyd Garrison, who began publishing *The Liberator*, in which he called passionately for the immediate emancipation of the enslaved. The great revivals of the Second Great Awakening deeply influenced the strident abolitionist call to repentance. Abolition was also in the news; in 1834, the British parliament abolished slavery in the British colonies. A £20 million settlement was given to former enslavers, and an apprenticeship system was created for formerly enslaved persons.

The new abolition movement began in earnest in New England. The atmosphere at antislavery meetings was like a religious revival. Methodist ministers like La Roy Sunderland and Orange Scott attacked slavery as a sin with high flung rhetoric. They cried out for repentance and conversion to abolitionism and demanded immediate emancipation.

Orange Scott was a gift to the nascent abolition movement among Methodists. Born to a Vermont day laborer, Scott had limited formal education, receiving only thirteen months of schooling by the time he turned twenty-one. He was converted to Christianity at a Methodist camp meeting and was licensed to preach within a year. He rose through the ranks to become a presiding elder in Massachusetts in 1830.

Scott knew little about slavery and didn't begin ministry as an abolitionist. He was introduced to it by a colleague who happened to be opposed to abolition. Scott spent a year reading and studying the movement before pledging his life to abolition in 1834.

The early abolition movement had hoped to provoke gradual change through a "brotherly reconciliation approach."[32] Methodists and other Evangelicals believed that slavery could best be eradicated by changing the hearts of individuals. New abolitionists like Scott fielded an unrelenting frontal attack on slavery and enslavers. Scott identified the evil of slavery in the absolute control of enslavers over other human beings, usurping the place of God. He tied his strong critique of slavery to the writings of John Wesley, often comparing Wesley's views with the current morally compromised views of the church. "Spirit of Wesley," he cried, "where hast thou fled?"[33]

One can see Orange Scott's rhetorical gifts on full display in a remarkable recollection by the Quaker poet and abolitionist John Greenleaf Whittier. Scott was in a debate, and an objection had been raised that abolitionists were "blinded by prejudice and working in the dark." Abolitionists

32. Emerson and Smith, *Divided by Faith*, 30.
33. Quoted in Morris-Chapman, "Methodist Responses," 47.

were often caricatured as wild radicals who cared only for the sound of their own voices.

Scott fired back: "'Blind though we be, aye, Sir, though blind as Samson in the temple of Dagon, like him, if we can do no more, we will grope our way along, feeling for the pillars of that temple which has been consecrated to the bloody rites of the Moloch Slavery; and, grasping at their base . . . o'erturning the supports on which this system of abomination rests, upheave the entire fabric, whose undistinguishable ruins shall yet mark the spot where our grandest moral victory was proudly won.'" Whittier concludes: "The climax was complete; the applause was unbounded as the speaker retired."[34]

While Scott had no personal experience with slavery when he began ministry in the church, he more than made up for it in the years that followed. He was an effective journalist and a powerful advocate against slavery in public halls, in churches, and at the church's larger gatherings at General Conference.

The General Conference Responds

The Methodist antislavery movement was a small but powerful lobby at the General Conferences of 1836 and 1840. In 1836, over against cries for immediate emancipation, the delegates declared their opposition, but not to slavery. Instead, they decided to oppose "modern Abolitionism, and wholly disclaim any right, wish, or intention to interfere in the civil and political relation between master and slave as it exists in the slave states of the union."[35]

This had become one of the main ways to shut down talk of abolition in the church without actually defending slavery. It was rooted in biblical passages like 1 Pet 2:13: "Submit yourselves for the Lord's sake to every authority instituted by men." Proslavery advocates took this verse quite literally to mean that the church was under the authority of the state in all civil matters. Some even confessed that while it was true that slavery was evil, the church could do nothing about it because it was none of the church's business.

Orange Scott and others argued that the distinction between the realms of the church and the state was arbitrary. It was always the right

---

34. Quoted in Matlack, *History of American Slavery*, 101–2.
35. Quoted in Mathews, *Slavery and Methodism*, 142.

of the church to oppose all sin. And to those who pressed the argument that "this abolition was not conducive to the peace of the church," Scott was quite frank: "It may not, perhaps, be always best, that the Church be at peace." Given that the MEC was in an "unholy alliance with slavery," there should be no peace until "she cleanses the skirts of her garments from 'blood guiltiness.'"[36]

The General Conferences of 1836 and 1840 failed to do anything about slavery. As decision after decision favored the southern cause, GC1840 even defended the right of ministers to enslave people if manumission was not possible in their state. Abolitionism seemed hopelessly sunk. When abolitionists attempted to address annual conferences, they were silenced by their bishops; in contrast, bishops of southern conferences did not silence the defenders of slavery.

Orange Scott, Le Roy Sunderland, and several others saw no alternative but to secede from the MEC. In 1843, radical Methodist abolitionists, numbering about six thousand, left the denomination to form The Wesleyan Methodist Connection. The new denomination, which spanned twelve states, was organized through a new church newspaper, *The True Wesleyan*, published by none other than Orange Scott. In their stated reasons for separation, they included not only slavery but the episcopacy, because, in conference after conference, they had watched with exasperation as bishops protected enslavers and shut down debate about abolition.

When Abolition Is Racist

Despite the best efforts of the early Methodists, racial discrimination became firmly embedded in American Methodism. Even in northern states, where slavery was illegal, racial segregation was practiced. And for many who opposed slavery, equality for Black persons was not on the table. The MEC was officially opposed to slavery, but early Methodists struggled to welcome Black persons into the church, often leaving them to listen through a window or out in a barn.[37]

We also find these dynamics at work in some abolitionists like Freeborn Garrettson, who may best be remembered as the pastor who traveled far and wide, gathering preachers for the Christmas conference held in

36. Matlack, *Life*, 92.
37. Morris-Chapman, "Methodist Responses," 44.

Baltimore in 1784.[38] Garrettson has also been revered as an abolitionist. He didn't come to abolition through reading antislavery books or hearing speakers at camp meetings, but in a spiritual experience. Inwardly, he said, God spoke to him: "It is not right for you to keep your fellow creatures in bondage; you must let the oppressed go free."[39] Which he did, becoming one of the first Methodist preachers to free those whom he had enslaved.

As Garrettson's views matured, he developed a two-pronged approach to ending slavery. He promoted a gradualist approach to emancipation. He also championed colonization as a way to separate the races, although his scheme was slightly different. Garrettson wanted to use the newly acquired Louisiana Territory as a refuge for free and enslaved Black people.[40]

Serious questions remain about how fully Garrettson bought into the equality of Black persons. He often preached to segregated Black and White audiences without comment. His belief in the inferiority of Black persons is revealed in a remark he wrote about colonization: "no doubt, a large proportion of them [Black persons] would rather stay with their White brethren, and be hewers of wood, and drawers of water for them."[41]

Garrettson modeled a conflicted understanding of the status of Black persons in the church and in society. In his passion for abolition, there was a clear recognition of the humanity of the enslaved. Alongside this recognition was the lingering belief that Blacks were not equal to Whites. We've seen this racist dynamic more blatantly at work in those who supported the colonization movement. But it was also present among many abolitionists, for whom emancipation was simply about freeing enslaved persons and not about integrating Black persons fully into the life of the church.

Like the fabled heads of Hydra, this paradoxical thinking about Black persons will endure far beyond this time and continue to trouble the church well into the twentieth century.

Yes, We Defend Slavery

When Methodist abolitionists sharpened their focus on immediate emancipation in the 1830s, this goaded Methodist proslavery forces in the South into action. The debate over slavery in the church had become incredibly heated

38. Many White abolitionists decried slavery, but would not accept Black equality.
39. Quoted in Straker, "Black and White," 19.
40. Straker, "Black and White," 22.
41. Quoted in Straker, "Black and White," 22.

and hyperbolic. Abolitionists argued that the southern Methodist mission to enslaved persons was "a demonic and grotesque misuse of the gospel."[42] Northern abolitionists were blasted by southern apologists as irrational and self-seeking in their dramatic oratory; they were subjects "of an infatuation of incalculable power both to fever the brain and chill the heart."[43] These missiles were volleyed back and forth through sermons, printed pamphlets, and articles in church magazines like (the northern) *Zion's Herald* and the *Southern Christian Advocate*. Abolitionist La Roy Sunderland faced several ecclesiastical trials for slanderous writing against enslavers.[44]

Another factor contributing to the relentless defense of slavery was the continuing rise of the "Cotton Kingdom" in the South in the early nineteenth century. Several technological improvements, including the perfecting of the cotton gin, produced incredible economic benefits for southern planters. As a consequence, the forced labor of those enslaved was pursued in ever increasing numbers to meet the worldwide demand for cotton.

In response to attacks from abolitionists, southern Methodists turned to the Bible for support, although their arguments commonly ranged across several fields—political philosophy, theology, and culture. For example, the idea that slavery somehow elevated those enslaved from their wretched lives in Africa persisted, as did fears that emancipation would lead to uprisings of the enslaved and bloodshed. Enslavers also contended that while they'd be more than happy to free their enslaved, state laws would not allow it. Historian Frederick Norwood, however, suggests otherwise. Freeing enslaved persons would take a good deal of work, but it was possible in almost every case. Norwood asks, "Were the supposed laws against manumission used by Methodists as an excuse for doing nothing?"[45] At GC1844, Peter Cartwright called it "humbuggery" when Bishop Andrew claimed he could not legally free those he had enslaved. On the Conference floor, Cartwright explained that he had once inherited enslaved humans: "I took them to my state, set them free, gave them land, and built them a house, and they made more money than I ever did by my preaching."[46] In contrast to his southern colleagues, Cartwright set over two hundred enslaved humans free!

---

42. Mathews, *Slavery and Methodism*, 179.
43. Quoted in Mathews, *Slavery and Methodism*, 18.
44. Norwood, *Schism*, 41.
45. Norwood, *American Methodism*, 204.
46. Quoted in White, "Antislavery Struggle," 39.

The primary arguments used by enslavers to commend slaveholding came from Scripture. We've already seen how they deployed Scripture texts about the duties of Christians to obey the civil authorities against the abolitionists. Texts about the subordination of women, such as 1 Tim 2:11–15, were turned to argue for the place of enslaved persons in southern society. Proslavery biblical polemics also relied heavily on the silence of the Bible on moral judgments about slavery. Abraham, the "father of faith," held enslaved persons seemingly without earning God's wrath. The Ten Commandments mentioned slavery twice without comment. Jesus never talked about slavery, and Paul returned Onesimus, a runaway, to his enslaver.

The most common justification for slavery, however, was grounded in what was called the "curse of Ham." This bewildering story, recorded in Gen 9, features Noah and his three sons. One of them, Ham, finds his father naked and drunk on the floor of his tent. Ham tells his brothers, who then grab a blanket and walk in backward to cover their father and avoid seeing him naked. When Noah sobers up, he curses Ham's son, Canaan, who will now be enslaved to his brothers.

Proslavery advocates claimed this story as divine authority for enslaving human beings. This was quite a stretch, given the shakiness of the biblical foundation. No one seemed to notice or care that it was Canaan who was cursed, not Ham, that there was nothing in the curse about race or color, nor that the punishment—the perpetual slavery of African persons—seemed to vastly outweigh the crime. What little there was in the Bible that might have caused them some discomfort over the southern institution of slavery—that slavery in the Bible was neither racially based nor was it chattel slavery—was conveniently ignored.

The Bible was also misused in other ways. William Capers, a prominent clergy from South Carolina, was celebrated as the founder of the MEC's evangelistic mission to enslaved people. Capers was able to overcome the fears of plantation owners over missions by arguing that "nothing is better calculated to render man satisfied with his destiny in this world than a conviction that its hardships and trials are as transitory as its honors and enjoyments."[47] The unstated implication, of course, was that the religious faith of the enslaved, with its promise of a blessed afterlife, would compensate for their continued slavery.

Capers further perverted the gospel by saying that Christian faith would lead directly to better enslaved persons. He even created a catechism

47. Quoted in Mathews, *Slavery and Methodism*, 71–72.

whose purpose was to indoctrinate those enslaved to understand that if they desired their eternal reward, they must obey their enslavers. One historian rightly labeled this as "Caper's false gospel of white supremacy."[48]

Although this may seem a bit strange for a pastor to confess, one of the grave difficulties that Christian abolitionists faced was that the Bible does not make a very strong case for abolition. Dozens of texts simply take slavery for granted. Some texts, particularly in the New Testament, make no moral comment on slavery other than urging compassionate treatment of those enslaved by enslavers and the obedience of the enslaved. There are precisely no texts that call for the emancipation of the ones enslaved.

This is a massive problem in our tradition—that the source of our faith is so uncritical of slavery—and one that is beyond the scope of this small book to address. But it's undoubtedly a reminder that the church must be ever vigilant at continuing to move beyond proof texting and, in the case of slavery, to "act on biblical teaching about the full humanity of all people, regardless of race."[49]

Of course, this is precisely what abolitionists were forced to do—to argue from general principles that all are created in the image of God, and that loving our neighbor is the chief commandment. They relied on stories like the good Samaritan (Luke 10:25–37) or texts like Gal 3:28 that pointed toward the end of slavery: "There is no longer Jew or Greek, there is no longer slave or free, there is no longer male and female; for all of you are one in Christ Jesus."

If we rely on a literal reading of a few selected texts in Scripture, we will never be able to reckon fully with racism and White supremacy in our tradition. But if we look at the trajectory of Scripture, taken as a whole, we find that it points away from a culture of slavery toward a world where all humans are created by God and are of infinite worth. If we look at the deeper principles in Scripture, it's clear that our model for relating to our neighbors, near and far, is the love of God, which works for the good of all humanity and against all that would diminish or degrade humanity.

The Inevitable: Division

During GC1836 the bishops were united in their condemnation of abolitionists: "We have come to the solemn conviction that the only safe,

48. Morris-Chapman, "Methodist Responses," 43.

49. Noll, *Theological Crisis*, 74.

scriptural, and prudent way for us, both as ministers and people, to take, is wholly to refrain from this agitating subject."[50] This seemed to be the prevailing direction of the church, toward an uncomfortable toleration of slavery and a shunning of those who opposed slavery. At GC1840, there was more of the same. The bishops stated that the only business of the church was "to promote the moral and religious improvement of the slaves" and not to interfere with their actual enslavement.[51] The clergy went so far as to pass a resolution declaring that "the simple holding of slaves . . . constituted no legal barrier to the election or ordination of ministers."[52] But GC1844 would change all that.

Conservatives, unwilling to side either with proslavery advocates in the South or abolitionists in the North, had essentially held the church together through these turbulent times. Their continuing refrain lifted up the spiritual value of church unity over the nitty-gritty of moral or political concerns. But slowly, their position in an untenable middle began to unravel. After southern apologists upped the ante both by defending slavery from the Bible and claiming that it wasn't a moral evil, conservatives could no longer support the South.[53]

To place GC1844 in a broader context, recall that a small contingent of antislavery supporters had left the church in 1843 to form the Wesleyan Methodist Connection. Talk of Texas annexation and the expansion of slavery was in the air. The question of whether enslavers could be bishops had popped up in the church. GC1844 would not be able to shuffle aside the issue of slavery for another four years.

On May 1, 1844, 180 delegates from thirty-three conferences representing over one million Methodists gathered at Greene Street Methodist Church in New York City to decide the fate of the MEC. Not that anyone is keeping records, but this Conference would prove to be one of the longest in Methodist history—six weeks! The main event was the status of Georgia bishop James O. Andrew, who had become an enslaver after his consecration as a bishop.

The delegates had a dry run with the case of a traveling preacher from Baltimore, Francis A. Harding, who was appealing his suspension for refusing to liberate enslaved persons he had gained through marriage. After

50. Quoted in Richey et al., *American Methodism*, 83.

51. Quoted in Culver, *Negro Segregation*, 48.

52. Quoted in Gravely, "Methodist Preachers," 219.

53. See Mathews, *Slavery and Methodism*, 212–13, 248.

three days of debate, delegates at GC1844 voted 117 to 56 in support of Harding's suspension by the Baltimore Conference. This was the first time southern Methodists had lost such an important decision, mainly because the conservatives had switched sides. Pandemonium briefly broke out at the announcement. William A. Smith, who had unsuccessfully defended Harding, lambasted the Conference, leading to a reprimand from the presiding bishop for his "disrespectful manner." All could see the writing on the wall: a schism in the MEC between the North and South was likely not far off.[54]

When GC1844 turned to the case of Bishop Andrew, Peter Cartwright, the legendary frontier preacher who was a delegate at the Conference, described the mood: "This fact came upon us with the darkness and terror of a fearful storm, and covered the whole General Conference with sorrow and mourning."[55] Andrew had reportedly been bequeathed enslaved persons through two marriages. Supporters argued for a distinction without a difference: that he did not own enslaved persons but was merely their trustee. The abolitionist view on the matter was unbending: if Andrews remained a bishop, then the church was no longer following its own rules against clergy enslaving people.

One resolution proposed that the bishop resign in uncompromising but colorful language: "and whereas it has been, from the origin of said Church, a settled policy . . . to elect no person to the office of Bishop who was embarrassed with this great evil. . . . Resolved that the Rev. James O. Andrew . . . is affectionately requested to resign his office."[56] Andrew was prepared to resign, but southern delegates protested his resignation. After nearly two weeks of meetings, a partial compromise was reached—that the bishop "desist from the exercise of his office so long as this impediment [enslaving] remains."[57]

No sooner had the vote been taken and counted in favor of the compromise than there was a protest against the decision, followed by a plan to divide the MEC. Reluctantly the General Conference adopted a plan of separation, and the Methodist Episcopal Church, South (MECS), was organized a year later in Louisville, Kentucky, making the MEC a strictly northern institution. Slavery, which was the fundamental dividing issue for

---

54. Quoted in Mathews, *Slavery and Methodism*, 253–54.

55. Quoted in Bucke et al., *American Methodism*, 2:54.

56. Quoted in Bucke et al., *American Methodism*, 2:55.

57. Quoted in Bucke et al., *American Methodism*, 2:57.

the church, was now allowed for both laity and clergy in the newly formed denomination. For the record, in the year before the division, southern Methodist laity had enslaved 208,000 human beings; 1,200 southern Methodist clergy were enslavers.

Southern Methodists, however, did not vote as a block. Rev. John Clark, who had transferred from Illinois to lead the Rutersville District (southeast of Austin) in Texas, was one of two Texas delegates to GC1844. After trying unsuccessfully to be excused from voting, Clark voted in favor of the resolution calling for Bishop Andrew's resignation, much to the dismay of the brand new Texas Conference. At the next session of the Texas Conference, Clark was denounced for misrepresenting the views of his conference and abusing their trust, making him deserving of the highest censure.[58] Fortunately for Clark, he had sent his family north for health reasons, and he joined them immediately after conference. He was warmly received into the Troy Conference in New York.

It would be fairly easy at this point to make moral judgments about southern Methodists who would sever the church over the right to enslave humans. This is why it's good to keep in mind this word from historian Forrest Wood: "Cynical though it may sound, it is not an exaggeration to submit that the critical fact in determining who opposed slavery and who supported it was . . . a consequence entirely of political and economic factors. All of the Christian conviction in the world could not dent the purse of one slaveholder."[59] To put it simply—it was much easier to decry slavery in the North than in the South. Likewise, it seems it was easy to miss how much the northern economy benefitted from the slavery of humans. Several wealthy families in America and Great Britain had built their fortunes on the backs of human slavery. What was often hidden in the heat of the debate was the way slavery had wrapped its tentacles around everything![60]

With the separation of the northern and southern churches, one might have guessed that much stronger antislavery legislation would be welcome in the MEC. Yet, for various reasons, slavery did not rise to the top of the agenda until the General Conference met in Indianapolis in 1856. That Conference was deluged with proposals and petitions on the question of slavery. When the Committee on Slavery reported, they urged that the

---

58. Vernon, *Methodist Excitement*, 75–76.

59. Wood, *Arrogance of Faith*, 276.

60. The fact that Methodism became more and more sectionally divided only contributed to divisions over slavery. See Richey et al., *Methodist Experience*, 1:100.

church tighten its rules to reflect its opposition to slavery. They wanted the *Discipline* amended finally to read that no enslaver be permitted membership in the church. This is something abolitionists had fought for over the last two decades.

Instead of stepping up to support the humanity of the enslaved and the inhumanity of slavery, the Conference decided that the report was unconstitutional and that it would not be good for the church. The same reasons for which southern Methodists had rejected more stringent rules about slavery had come to roost in the North: "Any increased stringency of the Discipline on the subject of Slavery, will greatly weaken, if not destroy our church in the slaveholding States, and along the border."[61] In spite of the split, the MEC still considered itself a national church. Antislavery activist Hiram Mattison wryly observed that "[we] are an 'antislavery' slaveholding Church!"[62]

Finally, in 1860, the antislavery forces pushed a strict rule through General Conference, admonishing both pastors and lay people to "keep themselves pure from this great evil [slavery], and to seek its extirpation by all lawful and Christian means."[63] While the new MEC rule condemned the buying, selling, and enslaving of people, it was declared advisory and could not be enforced. The MECS excised the General Rule which forbade trade in humans. In retrospect, one must wonder if there was all that much difference between northern and southern Methodists on human bondage in 1860.

Conclusion

We twenty-first-century Methodists must somehow come to terms with the fact that many nineteenth-century Methodists who were well versed in the horrors of slavery chose not to grapple with it at all and most days seemed perfectly at ease with it. Surprisingly, this was also true for a great many northern Methodists. Some Methodists in the South routinely supported slavery by turning to the Bible. One could argue that slavery could not have existed for so long without theological justification. Come wartime, many joined forces, even laying their lives on the line, to preserve this tragic institution.

61. Quoted in Bucke et al., *American Methodism*, 2:198.

62. Quoted in Bucke et al., *American Methodism*, 2:201.

63. Quoted in Graham, *Black United Methodists*, 31–33.

We must also face the failure of Methodists to do so little for those who were enslaved. There were clearly opportunities. At GC1828, for example, Peter Cartwright proposed that inhumanity toward the enslaved—insufficient food and clothing, cruel treatment, and family separation—be treated by the church as immorality. The motion was neither discussed nor voted on.[64]

Yes, there were courageous abolitionists in the church, like Orange Scott and LaRoy Sunderland, who stood for racial justice, and surely hastened the church's split. But many who opposed slavery thought abolitionists had gone completely off the rails and hoped slavery would just fade away.

Finally, very few in the MEC were willing to take what was then a "radical" move, namely, to support the full equality of Black persons. Racism—the superiority of Whites over Blacks—was so ingrained in the church that it was assumed and never seriously challenged. Hence, the decades prior to the Civil War essentially became the preface for what ultimately followed. As the authors of *Divided by Faith* put it, "By calling for an end to slavery but not racial division, the table was set for a large serving of Jim Crow."[65]

Questions for Discussion

1. Why did Methodists soften their antislavery stance after the formation of the Methodist Episcopal Church?

2. How important is numerical growth in attendance in comparison to progress on justice issues?

3. What circumstances led Richard Allen to form the African Methodist Episcopal Church? How important is it today for Black and White Methodists to worship together?

4. How was the Bible used to defend the existence of slavery? Do you see any parallels to this defense in our own time?

---

64. Mathews, *Slavery and Methodism*, 53.

65. Emerson and Smith, *Divided by Faith*, 33.

4

From Civil War to the Jim Crow Church

THE NORTH-SOUTH SPLIT OVER slavery in 1844 into the Methodist
Episcopal Church and the Methodist Episcopal Church, South, was a major
portent of the great division and deadly conflagration of the Civil War in
1860. Methodists were not alone; the Presbyterian Church and the Baptist
Church also divided well before the war. None of the church splits resolved
the problem of slavery. It could be argued that in the long run, neither did
the Civil War. Tragically, slavery morphed into the terrors of the Jim Crow
era (1877–1965).

Historian Jemar Tisby raises two key facts about the Civil War that
relate to our study of the church and race: "That the Civil War was fought
over slavery and that countless devout Christians fought and died to preserve it as an institution."[1] Southern White Methodists who worshiped God
on Sunday morning, put their very lives on the line on Monday morning
and signed on to a war that would maintain chattel slavery.

This is the virus-like quality of White supremacy: it infects and twists
the minds of otherwise moral persons. And this is also the continuing paradox of the White American Methodist Church throughout its history: the
proclamation of love of God and neighbor somehow believed and lived
alongside support of the inhuman bondage of Black persons, segregation,
and Jim Crow. A statement signed by religious leaders in the South, including prominent MECS leaders, attests to this incongruity: "We testify

---

1. Tisby, *Color of Compromise*, 71.

in the sight of God, that the relation of master and slave among us, is not incompatible with our holy Christianity."[2]

As we continue to trace the Methodist Church's struggle with race, we'll follow the path from war and reconstruction, up to the reunion in 1939. We'll begin with the developments within the larger church, both North and South, and then narrow our focus down to the church's response to the horrors of Jim Crow times.

War and Reconstruction of the Church

The Civil War had an enormous impact on all churches, not simply in terms of members lost in the war and property destroyed, but in the movement of Black members and the growth of Black Methodist churches. Historians point out that with emancipation and the end of the war, Black worshipers in White Protestant denominations used the occasion to flee the paternalism and social control of their former churches.[3]

Both during and after the war, the AME, the AMEZ, and the MEC sent missions to the South and gained Black members.[4] This was partly due to the massive Black membership exodus from the MECS, which declined from well over two hundred thousand to around twenty thousand in 1869. Why? Newly freed Black members wanted to run their own churches, and they desired freedom from increasing racial discrimination and segregation in southern Methodist churches.[5]

These jarring changes in church demographics provoked some to reflect on the causes. Had God indeed punished the southern churches for instituting slavery? Southern Methodists offered many reasons for the current shape of the church, but one that seemed to override the others was that the churches had not done enough to save the souls of the enslaved "entrusted" to them.

Consequently, their first response was a rededication to mission work among the now freed peoples. For the most part, that mission meant evangelism, not education; the idea of educating Black people remained an enigma to many southern White Methodists. Not surprisingly, the mission

2. Quoted in Richey et al., *Methodist Experience*, 1:119.

3. Shattuck, *Episcopalians and Race*, 8.

4. In the 1844 separation plan, the MEC had agreed *not* to organize churches in the South.

5. Norwood, *American Methodism*, 252.

was heavily paternalistic. Southern White Methodists believed God had chosen them to be the guardians of God's African children. Southern Whites should, in the jarring words of a writer in the *Southern Christian Advocate*, do all they could "to make what was the happiest and best class of slaves in the world to be the happiest and best class of peasants."[6]

Reconstruction also opened up new opportunities for churches in the North. Northern White Methodists raised funds, sent missionaries south to aid newly freed enslaved persons, and began furiously organizing churches. Some southern White Methodists referred to this movement disparagingly as the "Methodist Carpetbaggers." In 1864, after years of opposition and partly out of necessity, the MEC decided to ordain Black ministers. By 1870, the MEC counted ten conferences in the South, with 135,000 members, more than half of them Black members. Now that the church moved beyond its previous reluctance to ordain Black pastors, over half of the 630 pastors serving in the South were Black.[7]

These new conferences began their lives as mission conferences, a kind of stepchild to an annual conference. Even though, by the rules, they were not permitted to send delegates to General Conference, they elected delegates anyway! Now GC1868 was forced to decide what in the world to do with these new delegates before them. After ten days of debate, they voted overwhelmingly to raise the status of these mission conferences to annual conferences. Black Methodists were making it clear from the beginning that they were fully a part of the church!

After losing members both to the MEC and to the African Methodist denominations, southern Methodists headed in a different direction. At their GC1866, they formulated a plan to create a new church that would be a traditional alternative in the South for Black members. The not-so-hidden agenda of the MECS was to preserve the social order where everyone was in their place, and Black persons were subservient to Whites. Note that this blatant paternalism would not be limited to southern Methodists; we'll find as we move forward that it is a persistent underlying pattern in relations between Whites and Blacks in the whole church, both North and South.[8]

In 1870, the Colored (later Christian) Methodist Episcopal Church (CME) was formed with forty thousand members and five annual conferences. The new church adopted a rule that no White person was allowed

6. Quoted in Hildebrand, *Times Were Strange*, 9.

7. Norwood, *American Methodism*, 246.

8. Hildebrand, *Times Were Strange*, 11.

to become a member, whereas membership in the AME and the AMEZ was open to all. The CME remained closely connected to southern White Methodists, which brought much criticism from the more radical Black Methodist denominations for its ties to traditional southern ways. How could Black people join a church essentially birthed by a denomination that had enslaved humans?

By contrast, the African Methodist Churches (AME and AMEZ) were preaching a social gospel of liberation. Historian Reginald Hildebrand adds that these churches "emphasized the need for former slaves to free themselves from the control of Whites and become equal, independent, fully franchised citizens."[9] It's interesting to note that the growth of both African denominations was off the charts; by 1880, the AME Church had grown twenty-fold, the AMEZ Church fifty-fold, while the CME Church grew just three-fold.[10]

Changes in Education

With southern Methodists contributing little toward the education of the formerly enslaved, northern Methodists stepped into the gap with the creation of the Freedmen's Aid Society in 1866.[11] Within just a few years, the Society had created dozens of schools, orphanages, boarding schools, even colleges, including historic Black colleges.[12] Historian William B. McClain describes the creation of these colleges as one of "sacrifice, courage, love, heroism, and hope."[13] Many of these colleges began with limited resources; still, they performed "veritable miracles" in creating institutions that prepared leaders both for the church and the world. In the mid-1980s, when

9. Hildebrand, *Times Were Strange*, 33.

10. Hildebrand, *Times Were Strange*, 48.

11. There is some dispute over the date and the creation of the Freedmen's Aid Society. Methodists claim they birthed it in 1866, while the American Missionary Association claims to have founded it in 1861.

12. It's worth noting the names of these colleges that remain today: Bennett College, Greensboro, NC; Bethune-Cookman College, Daytona Beach, FL; Clark Atlanta University, Atlanta, GA; Claflin College, Orangeburg, SC; Dillard University, New Orleans, LA; Gammon Theological Seminary, Atlanta, GA; Huston-Tillotson College, Austin, TX; Meharry Medical School, Nashville, TN; Morristown College, Morristown, TN; Paine College, Augusta, GA; Philander-Smith College, Little Rock, AR; Rust College, Holly Springs, MS; and Wiley College, Marshall, TX.

13. McClain, *Black People*, 68–73.

McClain was writing his book *Black People in the Methodist Church*, fully 85 percent of the Black leaders in the Methodist Church had received their degrees from one of these twelve schools.

One might have assumed from the name that the mission of the Freedmen's Aid Society was specifically for those enslaved who had been recently emancipated. It certainly began that way, although the Society gradually shifted its priorities from Black to White southerners. This shift reflected the MEC's move to highlight missionary work among Whites, because they now had two hundred thousand White members in the southern MEC churches.[14] Within just a few years, twenty-one of forty-three Methodist schools were White. The goal of helping poor White families hurt by the war was a worthy one to be sure, so why not create an agency with that as its goal rather than raid the agency funded to help newly freed people?

With the advent of church-supported schools for both White and Black students in the years following Reconstruction, the question of interracial schools, or what were then called "mixed schools," surfaced. The MEC General Conference in 1884 landed on both sides of the issue. On the one hand, equal rights in education were strongly affirmed; on the other hand, segregated schools were allowed based on expediency and individual preference. What this meant in practice was that school administrations could do whatever they chose.[15]

The University of Chattanooga was founded as an all-White institution in 1886 with support from the Freedmen's Aid Society and private sources. When five Black students applied for admission, they were refused because it was deemed "inexpedient." The dean explained that if they admitted Black students, the White students would walk out. Abolitionist L. P. Cushman, who edited the *Southwestern Christian Advocate* (a Methodist newspaper), opined that "expediency" actually consisted of "ninety-nine planks of race prejudice and one of Christian brotherhood."[16]

Around the same time, a White faculty member at the university refused to shake hands with a Black pastor. That story attracted the eye of the press, moving the Freedmen's Aid Society into action. The Board of Trustees of the university was unwilling to comply with the Society's requests: to force the professor to resign and begin admitting Black students. The Society threatened to withdraw funding. The school had limited financial

14. Bennett, *Rise of Jim Crow*, 75.
15. Culver, *Negro Segregation*, 56–58.
16. Quoted in McPherson, *Abolitionist Legacy*, 275.

resources and acquiesced. However, when the school finally reopened, no Black students applied.

At this point, the story disappeared into the mists of history as the university relocated and changed its name, and the denomination reorganized its educational boards. In the larger church, freedom of choice for White students won the day, which in reality meant that the choices of Black students would be constrained, given that many schools weren't genuinely open to them at all.

This was a rocky time for the MEC as they attempted to navigate between the shoals of White racism and their own policies of equality and justice. We'll explore now in some depth the church's continuing struggles with integration.

The Anti-Caste Church

Reconstruction was a buoyant time for Black Americans as some moved briefly into elected office. New opportunities opened for them to start businesses and schools. However, this period was not without violence and all kinds of setbacks, including the persistence of segregation, discrimination, and violence. When Reconstruction abruptly ended in 1877, the rising tide of Jim Crow laws transformed race relations, bringing with it the loss of voting rights, continued policies of inequality, and growing violence and terror against Black Americans. While the MEC was generally in favor of equal treatment, by the late 1870s, race was unfortunately relegated to the back burner, partly out of hope for a reunion with the MECS.

Out of these precarious times emerged a new group of radicals led by folks like Gilbert Haven, one of the strongest and most vocal advocates for an interracial church. In 1864, he wrote: "The first, greatest, all absorbing duty of the Church is to secure the absolute oneness of all its members in Christ."[17] Following emancipation, the cause of abolition did not die but was resurrected in the form of anti-caste radicals like Haven. "Caste" was used by Methodists to describe a society ordered on the subordination and separation of one race from another.[18]

17. Quoted in Hildebrand, *Times Were Strange*, 86.

18. Isabel Wilkerson, in her book *Caste: The Origins of Our Discontents*, makes a case for understanding caste in America as a more fundamental category than race, because caste focuses on "keeping the hierarchy as it is in order to maintain your own ranking, advantage, privilege, or to elevate yourself above others or keep others beneath you," 70.

Haven was a pastor and editor of *Zion's Herald*, one of the oldest Methodist weekly magazines. Unafraid to enter the political arena, Haven, along with other pastors in the New England Conference, had fiercely opposed the 1850 Fugitive Slave Law, which required that enslaved persons be returned to their enslavers. Moving well outside the comfort zone of Methodists, North and South, he often preached on social equality between Blacks and Whites and even advocated for interracial marriage.

Haven understood that the unique mission of the church after emancipation was the creation of a racially integrated and just community. Separation or segregation in the church was "a scandal and offense, a stench in the nostrils of the Almighty."[19] Anti-caste radicals believed that a church transformed and fully integrated, having jettisoned the scourge of racial caste, would lead to the reformation of the country. Conversely (and prophetically), a church afflicted by separate churches for Black and White members would only lend more power to those who envisioned a thoroughly segregated world.[20]

Elected to the episcopacy in 1872, Bishop Haven made it clear from the beginning that he would act upon his racial views. The following year, he made a tour of the southern MEC conferences, leaving some of his colleagues to fear that his visit would be explosive! At the Holston Annual Conference (Eastern Tennessee, including parts of northern Georgia and southwestern Virginia), Haven canceled separate services for Black members and integrated worship. He ordained deacons and elders alphabetically rather than ordaining White candidates first.[21] One serendipity emerging from Haven's work was the dignity and confidence it gave Black pastors. Sadly, among White pastors and laity, he made few converts. His social witness was far ahead of its time.[22]

A crucial part of the argument White MEC members made in favor of integrated churches was theological. They charged those who favored segregation with being unfaithful to the inclusive message of Christ and to the witness of John Wesley. Haven frequently reminded Methodists that the church needed to recover the Pauline understanding of equality as seen in

19. Quoted in Gravely, *Gilbert Haven*, 127.

20. We should note here that Haven's conception of integrating churches was fairly rudimentary and paternalistic. He envisioned having Black churches and Black conferences simply join White ones. Gravely, *Gilbert Haven*, 132.

21. Gravely, *Gilbert Haven*, 207–8.

22. Hildebrand, *Times Were Strange*, 105.

Gal 3:28: "In that oneness, there shall be neither Greek nor Jew, barbarian nor Scythian, bond nor free."[23]

In response, southern Methodists took up a well-worn theme. They appealed to the doctrine of the spirituality of the church, arguing that matters of segregation were political matters. To preach and teach about these issues was, so they claimed, a forbidden practice in the Methodist Church.[24] Their own teaching which opposed even a hint of racial equality was somehow not political but "spiritual."

For a brief period following the Civil War, the MEC opposed the separation of conferences by race and attempted to live into racial inclusiveness. In fact, following the war, one of the prime reasons for the MEC's success in the South was that Black converts perceived that the MEC was anti-caste. Several annual conferences in the South had biracial memberships. Georgia formally organized its conference in 1867, justifiably proud of its work that brought together 8,000 Black and 2,300 White members.

GC1872 ruled that annual conferences could not be segregated along racial lines. But then, in a confusing reversal, as Reconstruction was coming to an end, GC1876 directed that Methodists could segregate their conferences with the consent of Black and White members in the conference. The motive? Northern Methodists knew that as the MEC pushed into the South, a biracial conference hindered increasing White membership.[25] With the GC1876 rule essentially blessing segregated conferences, all but three annual conferences had voted to separate by 1884.

There were, however, some illuminating exceptions. Bishop Edward Thompson presided over the inaugural session of the MEC Mississippi Mission Conference on Christmas Day, 1865, in New Orleans. The territory was impossibly large, covering Mississippi, Louisiana, and Texas, and the membership was tiny—nine congregations, five church buildings, and 2,216 members. Four men were to be ordained at this conference, three White and one Black. Reverend John P. Newman was appointed secretary of the conference and, watching this interracial ordination before him, wrote: "Was not this the commencement of a new era in the South?" The emotion in the room during the service was palpable, and the whole audience was affected, "some with tears, some with shouts."[26] The Mississippi

---

23. Quoted in Gravely, *Gilbert Haven*, 127.

24. Bennett, *Rise of Jim Crow*, 36–37.

25. Murray, *Crucible of Race*, 22.

26. Quoted in Hildebrand, *Times Were Strange*, 92.

Mission Conference maintained its biracial identity well into the 1880s, fully integrating both worship services and the communion rail.

The MEC Louisiana Conference, which came out of the Mississippi Mission Conference, included White and Black churches in the same districts, something peculiar to this conference. White and Black members met together, ate together, even stayed in each other's homes. However, these interracial gatherings were at the district or conference levels; congregations remained racially segregated.

Reverend Joseph Hartzell, a White pastor from the MEC, served churches and became a presiding elder[27] in the Louisiana Conference. His congregation, Ames Chapel in New Orleans, was one of the few integrated churches in Methodism. Throughout his ministry, he challenged racism and caste in the church and lifted up equality for Black church members and pastors.

Like Haven, he led by example. When he visited area churches as presiding elder, he stayed overnight exclusively in the homes of Black members. Once, when confronted by a church member who protested his invitation to a Black pastor to fill the pulpit, Hartzell fired back, "If I am forbidden to invite a brother minister to preach in my pulpit simply because his color was a shade darker than mine, my pastorate ends in that place."[28] The commitment of Hartzell and other Whites to racial equality was a great source of encouragement to Black members of the church who might have wondered whether the MEC was truly committed to being a biracial church.

I invite the reader to pause for a moment and wonder, "What if"? What if the rest of the Methodist Church had taken up this biracial identity? What kind of impact might a biracial church, as large and influential as the Methodists, have had in a country torn apart by racism and White supremacy? What if the Louisiana Conference had become the model for how the Methodist Church would be reconstructed? Imagine if our model for the church of the future drew from what happened in New Orleans following Reconstruction.

It would not have been an easy path. Real life in the biracial Louisiana Conference was anything but easy. Churches were burned. Black members were assaulted, and Black pastors risked death simply because they were leaders in an MEC church. Even White members faced hostile opposition, social ostracism, and public criticism, as did clergy. Some fared far worse.

27. This was equivalent to a district superintendent today.
28. Quoted in Bennett, *Rise of Jim Crow*, 24.

Eyewitnesses reported that a White teacher in rural Louisiana, who was also an MEC missionary, was taken out of his schoolhouse and beaten nearly to death by a mob in broad daylight. A five hundred dollar bounty was placed on his head, and a ten-day chase ensued. He reached safety in New Orleans and was able to continue teaching there.[29]

As the century came to a close, the church succumbed more and more to the White supremacist values of what was now a highly segregated society. Organizers of Methodist youth rallies, for instance, insisted on racial separation. In 1895, at the International Epworth League Conference in Chattanooga, Black youth delegates were asked to sit in a separate section at the back of the tent. An usher ordered them to move back, even threatened them with police arrest. An investigation revealed that the usher was not from the South, as had been presumed, but was an MEC member, and that the MEC organizers had approved the segregated seating to keep peace with the southern hosts.[30] All of this is also an important reminder that religious segregation in churches was not just a southern problem. Northern churches also acceded to segregation.

With integrated conferences fast disappearing, anti-caste radicals concentrated their energy on the election of a Black MEC bishop at the 1876 and 1880 MEC General Conferences.[31] The Conferences declined to elect a Black bishop, all the while affirming that "there is nothing in race, color, or former condition that is a bar to an election to the episcopacy."[32] Clearly this was true on paper, but not in practice!

The campaign for a Black bishop sputtered along until 1920. Black candidates for bishop had been on ballots for decades before 1920, but they never received enough votes. GC1920 circumvented this problem by creating a special election for two Black bishops. Robert E. Jones and Matthew Clair Sr. became the first Black Americans elected to the general superintendency of the MEC. The victory was not exactly a win for racial equality as the new bishops were limited to presiding over Black conferences.

Conditions for Black Americans continued to decline at the close of the nineteenth century under the harsh rule of Jim Crow. White people in power created new ways to subordinate Black people and resurrect the old

29. Bennett, *Rise of Jim Crow*, 26.

30. Bennett, *Rise of Jim Crow*, 78.

31. Prior to 1939 and the creation of jurisdictional conferences, bishops were elected by General Conference.

32. Quoted in Culver, *Negro Segregation*, 55.

southern social hierarchy. The various Black codes, laws, and customs of Jim Crow were most prevalent in the South, but they bled into the North as well. Two Supreme Court decisions played a critical role in supporting Jim Crow segregation. *Plessy v. Ferguson* authorized the doctrine of "separate but equal" and further empowered segregation in the South. *Williams v. Mississippi* essentially disenfranchised Black voters. Violence and terror were used to reinforce submission to these Black codes. Sadly, the Methodist Church, and especially the MECS, mirrored these oppressive conditions and maintained a vow of silence.

The Klan and the Methodist Church

The original Ku Klux Klan (KKK) was founded after the Civil War by Confederate veterans who used violence to keep Whites in power, intimidate Black persons, and combat Reconstruction. Nathan Bedford Forrest, a wealthy planter, slave trader, and lieutenant colonel in the Confederate Army, was the first leader of the Klan. From 1871 to 1873, Congress held hearings, gathering information and testimony about the activities of the Klan. The scope of their actions and the range of their violence was alarming. During the hearings, the story was told of Lewis Thompson, a Black Methodist pastor and a staunch Republican, who was warned not to preach in his church, located in Goshen Hill, South Caroline. A note was left for him in the pulpit with a drawing of his coffin on it. Thompson defied the order and was later lynched by the Klan right outside his home. By the grace of God, the first iteration of the Klan was short-lived, and with the end of Reconstruction in 1877, they disbanded.[33]

A former licensed MECS preacher, William Simmons, created the second incarnation of the Klan, inspired by D. W. Griffiths's 1915 racist film *Birth of a Nation*. The film blamed the country's problems on Republican policies, the "domination" by Black people, and racial intermarriage. Its public face was as a group dedicated to the ideals of patriotic, fundamentalist Protestant faith and White supremacy. But one didn't have to look very far to find its message of hate, which moved beyond targeting Black persons to include Jews, Catholics, and immigrants. The second Klan cleverly disguised its violence behind the cloak of parades, picnics, beautiful baby contests, and baseball teams. And, most important of all, behind the cloak of Christian (Protestant) faith.

33. *KKK 1871 Congressional Testimony*, 982, 994, 1031, 1182.

The 1920s Klan proved to be exceedingly popular. With the help of a public relations team, membership grew to somewhere between three and five million by the middle of the decade. Members were drawn from mainstream, middle-class America and included doctors, lawyers, bankers, and ministers. And lots of Methodists, both northern and southern.[34]

The leadership of the MEC was disappointingly quiet on the Klan. The General Conferences of 1920 and 1924 passed resolutions against "Klanlike" groups. Occasionally bishops spoke out, including one memorable scene where MECS Bishop W. F. McMurray punched one of his ministers in the mouth for supporting the Klan. (He was later charged with disturbing the peace.)[35] The Methodist press offered the most vigorous opposition, calling out the Klan with strong language. The *Northwestern Christian Advocate* denounced the Klan as abnormal and vicious, adding that any pastor who "refrains from denouncing an organization that plots its deeds in secret and executes its purpose cruelly and under mask, is not worthy to preach the gospel of an open-minded and clear-breasted Christ."[36]

For many, particularly in the South, it was easy to hide behind the so-called doctrine of the spirituality of the church in dealing with the Klan. Denouncing the Klan was considered a political act, and, therefore, outside the church's purview. Even if local leaders ginned up the courage to speak out against it, they did so at great risk to their lives. Consequently, the vast majority of churches (both local and conference gatherings), ministers, and lay leaders were silent.

The secrecy of the Klan makes it difficult to assess its influence on the Methodist Church. Without a doubt, there were Methodist churches scattered across the country that supported the Klan, had Klansmen within their membership, gave church space to Klan meetings, or pretended the Klan was not a threat to the social order. What is particularly distressing is that many pastors were involved as well. Historian Linda Gordon estimates that some forty thousand White Protestant ministers were members of the Klan, "and these people were sermonizing, regularly, explicitly urging people to join the Klan."[37]

Several Methodist pastors gave public support to the Klan, attracted by its claim to be about restoring law and order. Rev. H. D. Knickerbocker

34. Jacobson, "Silent Observer," 105–6.
35. Miller, "Note on the Relationship," 267.
36. Quoted in Miller, "Note on the Relationship," 358.
37. Quoted in Tisby, *Color of Compromise*, 102.

served as pastor of Methodist churches in Wichita Falls and Temple. He was also on the Board of Trustees at SMU and was finance director for the North Texas Annual Conference. In a guest sermon preached in El Paso, Knickerbocker made this incredible claim: "Justice may sometimes be rightfully administered outside the law. Jesus Christ did this when he took the cat o' nine tails and drove the money changers from the temple. In this respect He was the first Ku Klux Klansman."[38]

Alas, examples like this abound. Rev. W. E. Garrison, pastor of the Tahlequah Methodist Church in Oklahoma in the early 1920s, received a message from the Klan at the end of a worship service, hand-delivered by a group of thirty fully-robed Klansmen. The message greeted Garrison as an "Esteemed Friend" and continued with a rambling defense of the Klan and its purpose, "the preservation of American ideals and institutions and the maintenance of White supremacy."[39]

Fortunately, there were counterbalancing voices of reason, like Ralph Sockman, a northern Methodist pastor, who gained prominence as a writer and host of the weekly radio program *National Radio Pulpit*. Sockman was sure that sensible Protestants would reject the Klan because it was "a lawless organization using evil methods."[40]

That the Klan could coexist alongside the church, however, even co-exist inside the church, is continuing evidence of the stealthy way White supremacy had infiltrated Christianity. This allowed the Klan to stoke fear and terrorize marginalized communities over a decade or more and pass it off as somehow the way of Christ.

We turn now to two other ways that Whites in power terrorized the Black population—race massacres and lynching.

The Tulsa Massacre of 1921

At the end of World War I, there was a tremendous intensification of racial tensions due to an economic downturn, rising unemployment, and shifting demographics in the country. By 1919, an estimated five hundred thousand Black persons had emigrated from the South to the Northeast and Midwest for work in northern industries where there was an acute housing shortage. Major "race riots" began first in East St. Louis and Houston in 1917. These

38. Quoted in Jacobson, "Silent Observer," 107.
39. Agnew, "Klan."
40. Quoted in Miller, "Note on the Relationship," 366.

urban massacres, where Whites attacked Blacks, reached a bloody climax in 1919 when more than twenty-five cities in the North and the South descended into violence.

One of the worst happened on May 31 and June 1, 1921, in Tulsa, Oklahoma. Most accounts generally agree that the violence began with accusations of assault against nineteen-year-old Dick Rowland, a Black shoeshiner, who tripped and fell into seventeen-year-old Sara Page, a White elevator operator. Rowland was quickly arrested, and rumors spread that a mob was forming to lynch him. Upon hearing the news, seventy-five armed Black men, many World War 1 veterans, arrived at the courthouse to offer protection. An argument broke out, a shot was fired, and, like a match to kindling, mob violence exploded.

White rioters tore through the Tulsa neighborhood of Greenwood, often called Black Wall Street, destroying homes, looting businesses, and shooting residents. When the violence finally ended with the imposition of martial law, close to three hundred Black persons had died, ten thousand were left homeless, and twelve hundred buildings were destroyed.

It may not come as a complete surprise that when the presiding MECS bishop, E. D. Mouzon, preached in Tulsa the Sunday following the massacre, he blamed the violence on the victims. He began his sermon declaring that their Black friends must "understand that there can never be anything like social equality in America," even favorably quoting another bishop for support: "God Almighty has drawn the color line in indelible ink." Mouzon blamed the riot on the Black people in Greenwood and claimed that it could have been averted by the only real solution to racial tensions in America: following Jesus. A strange claim indeed, especially given the centrality of the church in Greenwood.[41]

Mouzon was not alone in his racist commentary. Sermons at other churches that morning in Tulsa echoed similar rants, almost as if they were reading boilerplate text. At First Methodist Church, Rev. J. W. Abel wondered aloud, "What other nation in all human history has done as much . . . as the White race has done for their race which but a brief half-century ago emerged from slavery?"[42] In many Methodist churches around the country, the response to racial riots between 1917 and 1921 was the same as the city of Tulsa. Silence. For decades, Tulsa covered up the horror of those two

41. "Tulsa's Race Riot."
42. Quoted in Ross, "Tulsa Race Massacre."

days until the late 1990s, when a state commission was finally formed to investigate the massacre.

For the church, the resounding silence of White supremacy is the space into which we are continually invited to speak the truth. One hundred years later, churches are finally stepping up. Boston Avenue UMC in Tulsa has begun work on a racial justice initiative that encompasses a whole host of actions "which foster racial reconciliation and bring forth justice and repair for any harm done by the church based on past or present deeds."[43]

The Horror of Lynching

The Equal Justice Initiative (EJI), founded in 1989 by Bryan Stephenson to provide legal representation to those who have been denied a fair trial, has taken on a remarkable project. It has documented over forty-four hundred terror lynchings in the United States from the end of Reconstruction in 1877 to 1950. Terror lynchings were horrifying acts of torture and violence on Black bodies carried out by White people to dominate and control Black persons. They were often in public, attended by overflowing crowds of onlookers from the White community. The perpetrators were never held accountable; the victims were murdered without even a nod to due process of law.

Part of EJI's work has been to break the silence over lynching and confront this awful history through conversation, memorials, and teaching. Part of our work as Methodists is not only to recognize the pain and horror of lynching but to come to terms with the role we played in allowing it to fester for so long.[44]

The causes of lynching were deeply rooted in a complicated mythology that wrapped together fear over racial intermixing, patriarchal control of White men over White women, and myths about Black male sexuality. In the 1890s, Ida B. Wells, an investigative journalist and a Methodist, called out what she named the "old threadbare lie" that had long supported lynching, that it had been used to punish Black men who had raped White women. More recent studies have shown that the true victims were overwhelmingly Black women raped by White men.[45]

43. "Boston Avenue."
44. *Lynching in America.*
45. Quoted in Hall, *Chivalry*, 149.

The response of the Methodist church to lynching was mixed. Some southerners supported lynching, while others expressed a much more ambivalent position. In the 1880s, MECS Georgia Bishop Atticus Haygood stood out from the pack with his strong stance against lynching, but he also accepted the claims of attacks on White women as true. Haygood is often grouped with the "uplift" movement, church folks in the South who insisted that rather than take away the Black vote, they should be about educating Black persons, all the while maintaining segregation.[46] Surely by now we have come to recognize the contradiction between trying to "uplift" and educate Black persons while supporting segregation.

At the local church level, while there were individuals who spoke out, indifference reigned. Keep in mind that between 1919 and 1939, lynching was not a rarity; there were over five hundred lynchings across the South. The witness from the pulpit was most often silence. In 1935 close to five thousand pastors in the South responded to a questionnaire which determined that fewer than 5 percent had preached about lynching or written to their congressional representative urging a federal anti-lynching law.[47] Even if these pastors had disagreed vehemently with lynching, going against the grain of hardened Jim Crow assumptions about Black Americans would have been extraordinarily difficult.[48]

The MEC unequivocally condemned lynching in the strongest terms as an "unpardonable blight" at GC1892 and in every conference thereafter. Although several MECS bishops condemned lynching, in general, southern Methodists were much more reticent and slow to speak out.[49] In 1922, the Episcopal Address at their General Conference condemned lynching and urged both pastors and laypeople to do all within their power to prevent outbreaks of mob violence in their communities and bring the instigators to justice.

Finally, in 1930, the MECS officially condemned lynching and mob violence. The immediate cause of this legislation was the horrific death of George Hughes, who had been jailed after pleading guilty to assaulting

---

46. Murray, *Crucible of Race*, 20, 29; Kenaston, "Methodists and Lynching," 30.

47. Miller, "Protestant Churches," 120.

48. One of the most remarkable sermons from this time condemning lynching was by Hawley Lynn, pastor of Grace Methodist Church in Pickens, South Carolina, entitled "Who Lynched Willie Earle?" Will Willimon, in his book *Who Lynched Willie Earle?*, provides the text of the sermon, the context of the horrific event, the reactions to it, and his own reflections as a homiletician.

49. Kenaston, "Methodists and Lynching," 33.

a White woman. The lynching occurred at the courthouse in Sherman, Texas, just north of where the MECS General Conference was meeting in Dallas. An unruly mob, undeterred by rounds of tear gas, set fire to the courthouse, and Hughes, locked inside, perished in the flames. The mob then proceeded to demolish much of the surrounding Black neighborhood, including homes and businesses. As news of the grotesque details of Hughes's murder spread through the Conference, the agenda for the day shifted to a resolution on lynching.[50]

In a study of racial violence and the MECS in this period, Connor Kenaston lifts up several reasons why the MECS finally condemned lynching. Chief among them were the grassroots efforts of Methodist women in the MECS.[51] We'll now take a deep look at their work to improve race relations and, most importantly, to end lynching.

Methodist Women Respond!

In the first two decades of the twentieth century, several groups were responsible for moving the needle forward on race relations, including the National Association for the Advancement of Colored People (NAACP), the National Association for the Advancement of Colored Women, the Young Women's Christian Association (YWCA), and the Commission on Interreligious Cooperation (CIC). Into that mix came the MECS Women's Missionary Council (WMC), influenced by the social gospel movement, who began work for justice with their Black neighbors in the South.[52]

Methodist women had been gathering since the Civil War to plan and carry out home and foreign mission work. Emboldened by the conviction that God's love and justice were for everyone, northern Methodist women founded missions in China, India, Brazil, and other nations. As the twentieth century opened, both northern and southern Methodist women began home mission work with Black women in the South. Bear in mind that women's leadership in the MEC and MECS churches was severely limited— for example, women were not seated at General Conference until 1922 and could not be ordained until 1956.

---

50. Kenaston, "Methodists and Lynching," 21–22.

51. Kenaston, "Methodists and Lynching," 22–23.

52. The WMC was a forerunner to the United Methodist Women, now United Women of Faith.

In many ways, Methodist women were ideally suited to make a difference in race relations. Frustrated by gender roles of the time, they were eager to get out in the world, live out their faith, and make a difference. They were guided by their reading and study, which was an integral part of their program. Increasingly, due to the influence of the social gospel movement, their readings included the analysis of social issues—poverty, temperance, race, and education. They were also autonomous and, therefore, not officially under the thumb of the larger church, which gave them considerable freedom in their work. Finally, they benefitted from the strength of the Methodist connection in the South, and the fact that there were women's groups in churches in every village and hamlet.

In 1914, Lily Hammond, a Methodist woman from Georgia, wrote an analysis of race relations, which was quite influential in this burgeoning women's movement. In her book, *In Black and White*, she departed from stereotypical views and challenged racial prejudice, tenant farming, sharecropping, and lynching. Hammond urged White women to move beyond charitable work with Black neighbors and engage in interracial friendships.[53] She confronted prejudice and injustice and rooted her views in the theological affirmation that all are created in the image of God. However, she did not directly take on segregation or White supremacy, which made her work more palatable for her White southern readers. Still, her work was so ahead of its time that her husband was forced to resign as president of Paine College in Augusta, Georgia. At the center of this interracial work, from the very beginning, were Black women from a growing Black middle class who began to meet and work together on projects of "racial uplift" as educators, community organizers, and social workers. Methodist women followed their lead, working as home missionaries, creating schools and settlement houses in Black neighborhoods.

Estelle Haskin and Carrie Parks Johnson, leaders within the WMC, organized deeper interracial work, including studies, dialogue, and community development projects. That work grew at a fantastic pace and included endeavors like establishing a clinic or a nursery for Black neighbors, giving talks on sanitation, creating new parks and playgrounds, and working toward bettering schools for Black students. Given the stiff opposition that their interracial missions often generated, the range of it all seems even more remarkable.[54]

---

53. Knotts, *Fellowship*, 46–48.

54. Methodist women were indirectly liberating themselves in their work from a

Will Alexander, a young activist and a southern Methodist pastor, was also a key figure in organizing work on racial relations in this period. He helped overcome skepticism among his cohorts at the CIC and coordinated a women's conference in Memphis in October 1920. About one hundred women from various women's organizations, including the WMC, were addressed by four Black women about their work in the Black community and the crushing weight of life under Jim Crow. They urged White women to challenge the malevolence of lynching. The final speaker, Charlotte Hawkins Brown, threw down the gauntlet to the assembled women: "So far as lynching is concerned if the White women would take hold of the situation, lynching would be stopped."[55]

It's worth noting that amid their success, Methodist women's groups continued to struggle with paternalism and racist stereotypes. For example, Charlotte Hawkins Brown was introduced at a CIC meeting with these words: "I cannot say any more, Mrs. Brown, for your race today than . . . that you are as fine as was my Negro mammy."[56] With all of the interracial work they had undertaken, it's a bit surprising that ending segregation never surfaced. Even in a group of socially progressive women, the grip of Jim Crow was fierce.

Still, exceptional women leaders emerged. Jesse Daniel Ames grew up in central Texas and cut her teeth in the temperance movement. She heard the clarion call from Charlotte Hawkins Brown to end lynching and responded with her superb organizing skills and her single-minded focus. The WMC had condemned lynching in 1913 and had done research to understand the facts, prevent mob violence, seek ways to bring the perpetrators to justice, and work on anti-lynching legislation. Ames decided it was time for a new tactic, a focus on a single issue: lynching. We should note that Ames did not initiate this movement; she drew on the decades-long work and experience of Black women who had struggled for years against lynching.

---

patriarchal environment. And they found a measure of freedom from the male-led Board of Mission in the Women's Division of Christian Service. Many southern women likely joined in an amen chorus when Maria Gibson, President of Scarritt College, offered this prayer at a 1926 meeting of the Women's Division: "Dear Lord, we pray for the men of the Board of Missions. Thou knowest how they have troubled and worried us. They have been hard to bear sometimes, but we thank thee that they are better than they used to be." Murray, *Crucible of Race*, 65.

55. Quoted in Hall, *Chivalry*, 93.

56. Quoted in Hall, *Chivalry*, 101.

With support from several women's groups, Ames and eleven other White women from various denominations formed the Association of Southern Women for the Prevention of Lynching (ASWPL) in 1930. Their stance toward lynching in their pledge was powerful and unequivocal: "We declare lynching is an indefensible crime, destructive of all principles of government, hateful, and hostile to every ideal of religion and humanity, debasing, and degrading to every person involved."[57] They rejected not only the myth of White allegations of rape, so often used to justify lynching, but also the underlying notion that White women were vulnerable and in need of protection.[58]

The genius of the ASWPL was that Ames didn't need to create a new organization; instead, the leadership used all of the existing networks of southern women to combat lynching in their communities. They drew support from many religious and civic groups, but their strongest support came from the WMC and southern Methodist women. Women were asked to sign a pledge to speak out against lynching as a crime; by the early 1940s, over forty-three thousand had signed on.

Their work took them into local communities where they conducted investigations and reported the tenuous connection between the facts of the lynching and what was published in the press. Against strong opposition, they labored to change the sensationalist way newspapers presented lynching. Ames noted a shift in reporting by the mid-1930s as journalists swung over to support the ASWPL.[59] In addition, the women sought pledges from sheriffs to eradicate lynching; by 1939, they had gathered the signatures of over twelve hundred peace officers. A similar campaign with governors in the South had all thirteen southern governors committed to the ASWPL's program to end lynching.

Southern White women like Dorothy Till also took on the risky business of direct confrontation with mobs. Will Alexander announced that "when White women appeared on a scene like that, these White men were afraid of them."[60] This courageous and dangerous work had a significant impact. In 1968, sociologist John Shelton Reed studied lynchings from

---

57. Quoted in Pinar, *Racial Politics*, 545.
58. Hall, *Chivalry*, 163–64, 180.
59. Barber, "Southern Women," 384.
60. Quoted in Barber, "Southern Women," 385.

1919 to 1942 and found that in the counties where the ASWPL was most active, there was a dramatic decrease in the number of lynchings![61]

As the decade wore on, southern Methodist women left the doctrine of the spirituality of the church behind and encouraged women to help shape public opinion. WMC leader Bertha Newell showed how nonsensical it was to separate the personal from the public sphere. She wrote that "every public issue with a moral content *has a direct bearing on our personal lives.*"[62] With that new orientation toward politics, one might have expected that the ASWPL would have strongly supported anti-lynching legislation at the federal level. But for several reasons, they didn't. ASWPL leader Jessie Ames argued that a federal law would not be enforced; only education and changed minds would end lynching. She also feared a backlash against Black men if a new law passed. The preference of Black women for a federal law led them to separate from the ASWPL. A Senate filibuster ultimately decided the fate of that bill. It would be almost one hundred years before lynching was made a federal hate crime when President Biden signed The Emmett Till Antilynching Act of 2022.[63]

Following the lead and working alongside Black women, Methodist women like Belle Bennett, Louise Young, Jessie Daniel Ames, Bertha Newell, and Carrie Parks Johnson provided significant leadership not only on the anti-lynching campaign, but on interracial meetings and projects. Their work gradually moved from charity to justice and from being centered in their own experience to being centered more fully in the experience of Black persons and families. Methodist women broadened the scope of their race relations work into schools, sanitation, health, and rural development. Christian Leadership schools allowed Black and White women to gather and share concerns that shaped their mission work.

Alice Knotts, in her history of Methodist women and race, argues that this movement of women was "one of the largest, longest, most far-reaching and underreported aspects of the civil rights movement in the United States."[64] We'll return to their work in the next chapter as they move more fully into challenging segregation and ending racial barriers.

61. Hall, *Chivalry*, 236.

62. Quoted in Knotts, *Fellowship*, 82.

63. Hall, *Chivalry*, 243, 246.

64. Quoted in Knotts, *Fellowship*, 19.

We Create a Jim Crow Church

In April 1939, delegates from three churches—the MEC, the MECS, and the Methodist Protestant Church (MPC)—met in Kansas City, Missouri, to unite into a new denomination. Planned for decades, the Uniting Conference had as its goal the creation of what would be the largest Protestant church in the country. Fraternal greetings were received from no less than President Roosevelt who lauded the Conference as "a harbinger of better things."[65]

The proposed "Plan of Union" would bring together under one roof all three churches, but it would also place all of the Black Methodist churches in a segregated body, called the Central Jurisdiction (CJ). When the vote was finally announced, and the plan was adopted, the delegates stood and sang the rousing hymn "We're Marching to Zion." But not all of the delegates. Back in a corner of the room, the Black delegates did not stand and sing. Many openly wept.[66]

How did the church get to this place? Was this truly a Jim Crow church, a capitulation to the times? Or was it a necessary transition toward fuller inclusion? We'll spend this section unfolding the story of the creation of the CJ.

In the decades prior to 1939, various northern and southern Methodist groups had talked about reuniting the church. Those conversations seemed to be driven by two factors: the desire for greater unity in the church spurred on by the new ecumenical movement and their hope to create the largest, most powerful Protestant denomination in the country. Note that even though there had been much healing between northern and southern Methodists, the unification plan was created against the backdrop of a particularly turbulent time in race relations.

When they did meet, it's not difficult to imagine the main stumbling block to union: what to do with nearly 350,000 loyal Black Methodists? From the start, southern Methodists proposed that Black members should voluntarily leave the MEC either to form a separate church or join the AME or AMEZ churches. This would be a hard sell for most northern Methodists. A second approach was to create a separate conference, a missionary conference, for Black Methodists. Neither of these plans seemed to recognize Black persons as full members of the new church. And simply bringing all of the Black churches into the union church was a non-starter for the MECS.

---

65. Bucke et al., *American Methodism*, 3:458.

66. McClain, *Black People*, 75.

Although it took almost three decades after it was first proposed to move forward, the idea of a separate jurisdiction for Black Methodists emerged as the only solution that both northern and southern Methodists could agree on. The new church would have six jurisdictional conferences: five were based on geography, one was based on race. Their primary responsibility was the election and support of bishops. The new CJ would have full representation at General Conference. They would also have representation on the various church boards and agencies, and they would elect their own bishops. However, for all purposes other than the general church connection, Black members would be completely segregated from the White membership. Methodists were so segregated already that it was not uncommon for White Methodists to be clueless that the Black church on the other side of town was not only Methodist but also part of their own denomination. We should also note that the jurisdictional system as a whole was not simply segregationist but racist since it was explicitly designed to preserve regional "culture" and "values," code words meaning that a Black bishop would never be sent South!

I. G. Penn and Robert E. Jones, who later became a bishop, represented Black churches in the deliberations. Initially, Jones had dismissed the idea of a separate jurisdiction for Black members. At one meeting in 1934, he said that "a Georgia legislature would not pass as discriminatory an act as this paper."[67]

Over time it became clear that the MEC and the MECS were determined to unite, come hell or high water. Both Penn and Jones shifted their support in favor of the jurisdiction plan. Jones said, "I do not want to be an obstructionist."[68] And they didn't want any failure to unite blamed on Black Methodists. Furthermore, Black members comprised about 5 percent of the Methodist Church, so they had little power to change the outcome.

When Penn and Jones announced their support for the jurisdictional plan, they were roundly condemned by the Black press. They shot back that this plan was the best that could be done. One wit remarked sarcastically in the *Southwestern Christian Advocate* (a Black Methodist publication): "An Omnipotent God has not yet made the White race perfect in race attitudes and relations. We cannot do more than God has done."[69]

---

67. Quoted in Murray, *Crucible of Race*, 38.
68. Quoted in Murray, *Crucible of Race*, 39.
69. Quoted in Murray, *Crucible of Race*, 39.

When it came time to vote on the plan, GC1939 approved it, 470 to 83; by contrast, Black delegates voted heavily against it, with thirty-six nays and eleven abstentions. Ratification of the plan by the annual conferences followed, and the pattern was the same. White conferences approved it almost unanimously; in Black conferences, it fared poorly, with 59 percent of the clergy and 64 percent of the laity rejecting it. One MECS conference—North Mississippi—voted it down. Apparently, even a separate jurisdiction would not remove Black members far enough away for their liking!

Of course, segregation had existed in the Methodist Church before 1939. Historian Ian Straker argues that in the immediate post-Civil War period, the separation of races was an accommodation to differences in worship styles, sensibilities, education, and training among the newly freed peoples. The CJ, though, was different because it was an accommodation to the racism long cultivated in the MECS. And now that segregation was sanctioned as official denominational policy, it would have ramifications far beyond the church in shoring up the segregation of the southern culture. Straker sums up the result strikingly: "For White and African-American Methodists who believed that the church should model for the world new possibilities of human fellowship and Christian harmony, a capitulation to racial intransigence was—and still is—a cause for weeping."[70]

In the northern church, some Whites were concerned about the ethical implications of the CJ, but most seemed to favor it as the best solution for the time. This should not have been surprising, given that full equality between Whites and Blacks was never on the table during consultations on a unity plan. Some White southerners were not quite ready to reunite with their northern brethren. They feared that it would not be long before there was intermixing of the races in their churches. A small group joined the new Southern Methodist Church, whose cornerstone appeared to be segregation.

Many progressive Methodists opposed the jurisdictional plan, including Mary McLeod Bethune, the daughter of formerly enslaved persons and a significant leader in higher education and civil rights. Methodist women working through the WMC also rejected the jurisdictional plan. Holding on to the inclusive gospel of Jesus, the women's report advised the church "to refuse to surrender the claims of Jesus to the comfort of traditional patterns."[71] In creating the CJ, the WMC insisted that the General

70. Straker, "Central Jurisdiction," 59.
71. Quoted in Knotts, *Fellowship*, 86.

Conference had caved in to the White supremacy that permeated both the northern and southern churches.

The report of the WMC was not far off the views of many Black Methodists. While there were some who supported the plan, the majority would have agreed with the assessment of David D. Jones, President of Bennett College: "Everyone knows the plan is segregation, and segregation is the ugliest way, because it is couched in such pious terms . . . it sets [people] aside, it labels them, it says that they are not fit to be treated as other people are treated."[72]

Given their history as Methodists, and now with the creation of a Jim Crow church, why did so many Black Methodists remain in the church? Many simply wanted to stay in the church of their birth. As William B. McClain has often said, "There has never been a time when Black people were not part of the Methodist Church."[73] It made sense, then, to give this new imperfect union a chance to work, in the confidence that the new Methodist Church (MC) was still committed to racial justice, despite appearances. Some hoped that the CJ would be temporary, a bridge to an integrated church of the future, although that future was absolute anathema to southern Methodists. In the end, though, what choice did they have? From 1939 forward, it was clear that Black Methodists either needed to join up with the uniting church and accept the CJ or leave. As historian John Graham put it in his book on Black Methodism, "The Negro became the 'sacrificial lamb' on the altar in order that union could be consummated."[74]

What About Northern Methodists?

One of the myths about racism we carry with us is a simplistic story of what racism looked like throughout the historical periods we've covered. It begins with the notion that racism was firmly located in one part of the country, the South. They were the enslavers, the segregationists, the White supremacists, the sinners. The North were the folks who saved the day: the abolitionists, the anti-racists, the freedom fighters, the saviors. During the debates at GC1966 over the Omnibus Resolution (which called for the end of any structures in the church based on race), K. Morgan Edwards, a delegate from California, argued that racism was not simply a southern

72. Quoted in McClain, *Black People*, 79–80.

73. McClain, "Historic Roots."

74. Graham, *Black United Methodists*, 90.

issue: "Those of us who are in the far West will one day have to stand before the judgment bar of God and accept heavy responsibility for the real estate conspiracies, the lack of economic opportunity and all the things which we did which produced the Watts riots." "Prejudice," he said, "belongs just as much to those of us in the West and the North as it belongs to anybody in the South."[75]

For one thing, if racism is genuinely systemic, then by definition it must be found in every part of the country. While northern society was not as closed as southern society, Black people who moved north during the Great Migration found similar patterns of discrimination, segregation, and racism in the North. And this discrimination was not simply *de facto*; it was often *de jure*. As Edwards alluded to above, following the Great Migration (1916–70), restrictive covenants were drafted all over the North, designed to keep Black people out of White neighborhoods.

The oft-quoted example of racism in the North is the awful story of Eugene Williams, who, on July 27, 1919, was swimming on the shore of Lake Michigan. He swam across an invisible line in the water—in the North, there were commonly no "White only" or "colored" signs—into an area reserved for Whites, only to be brutally lynched by a White crowd. This ignited thirteen days of rioting in Chicago that left twenty-three Blacks and fifteen Whites dead.[76]

Carolyn Renée Dupont suggests what may have led to the mythology that a more progressive North called a resistant White South to order: "[The] northern clerical presence in civil rights initiatives offers an image that bolsters this impression." What is overlooked is that liberal northern pastors who went south "appear not to have fully represented the sentiments of their home communities." Their parishioners were often more like their southern White counterparts who valued White rights over equal treatment of Blacks.[77] Even as I've traced a narrative that focuses mainly on racism and White supremacy in the South and in the MECS, we need to be clear that racism and White supremacy knew/know no bounds.

75. Quoted in Hawkins, *Bible Told Them*, 109, 112.

76. Wilkerson, *Warmth*, 272–73.

77. Dupont, *Mississippi Praying*, 182–83.

Conclusion

While the MEC seemed to gain some momentum following the Civil War toward desegregating the church, it was short-lived. As Whites regained political power in the South, segregation became the default for church and society. In what proved to be a repetition of past behavior, debates about segregation were shut down at General Conference.

The church struggled with segregation, both in the structuring of the church, in church-related colleges, and at church gatherings. By 1939, the long history of segregation within the church seemed only to contribute to the ease with which White Methodists embraced the Central Jurisdiction and officially segregated the national church. Several historians have suggested that the creation of a segregated church served to strengthen Jim Crow. If the moral authority of the church was not compromised by segregation, then neither was the nation's.[78]

Jemar Tisby has rightly observed that, after the Civil War, "racism never goes away, it just adapts."[79] Slavery was replaced by Black codes, segregation, economic exploitation, loss of voting rights, and continued violence. Likewise, the compromised response of the church to White supremacy adapted as well which explains the often tepid, mostly non-response to lynchings and the work of the Klan.

In the period following the Civil War, several other patterns emerged. First, White Methodists, mainly in the South, created a doctrine of the so-called "spirituality of the church," which became the standard response to segregation or Jim Crow laws. The church, so the argument goes, has everything to say about salvation and the state of one's soul, but nothing to say about political matters like segregation. (Of course, one could argue that segregation is very much a spiritual matter, and some did.) The corollary of this doctrine is that racism will only be cured by converted hearts. We'll find that this "doctrine" will continue to be wielded by the church as a free pass out of difficult conversations about racism as a systemic problem.

Second, we find a growing chasm between the local church membership and the leadership of the larger church. This meant that taking a firm stand on a social justice issue, say, against racism or White supremacy, would not come from local churches, lay people, or pastors but from the

---

78. Davis, *Unification*, 131.

79. Tisby, *Color of Compromise*, 110.

national level of the church, from the General Conference and national board executives, and sometimes from bishops and national periodicals.

Third, the direction of the MC was often captive to cultural models of success. In the quest for a larger membership, values were compromised. Leaders could conveniently ignore growing segregation and racism in church structures because to do otherwise would harm the greater "mission" or the unity of the church.

Finally, we observe some welcome divergence from previous patterns of compromise. More Methodists in this period emerged willing to face the racism in the church built by their ancestors, acknowledge the harm, and take steps to repair it. Individuals like bishops Haven and Hartzell in the MEC and groups like the Methodist women in the MECS forged a new path against often powerful opposition. But on the whole, our collaboration with racism continued unabated. Methodists somehow made peace with segregation and Jim Crow or ignored the growing racial terror all around them. We present-day Methodists must not only come to grips with this awful, painful history but also face up to the underlying theology that supported racial inequities and continues to dog us to this day.

Questions for Discussion

1. Following the Civil War, the MEC rededicated itself to mission work among the newly freed enslaved persons. Why? How was racism evident in the way these ministries were conducted?

2. How did the post-Reconstruction MEC struggle and generally fail to integrate? Why did some efforts succeed while others were abandoned? What are your thoughts on the "union" of 1939?

3. Why do you think White Methodist Women were the ones to take the strongest stand against lynching and anti-Black violence? What struck you as most significant about their work?

4. How would you explain the 1939 union and the creation of the Central Jurisdiction to a young person?

5

Methodists and the Civil
Rights Era (Part One)

ON MARCH 29, 1964, Easter dawned warm and bright in Jackson, Mississippi. Charles Golden and James Matthews arrived at the front door of Galloway Memorial Methodist Church, the largest Methodist church in Mississippi, to attend the 11 am worship service. Golden and Matthews were Methodist bishops, Golden in the Central Jurisdiction and Matthews in the Northeastern Jurisdiction. Golden had grown up in Mississippi and knew well that integrated groups had previously been barred from worship at Galloway. But it was Easter. Surely the doors of a Methodist church would be open to all?[1]

As they approached the church, they could see that ushers were closely guarding all the entrances. Nat Rogers, chair of Galloway's official board, met the bishops on the front steps. He explained, almost apologetically, that their current church policy did not allow them to admit Black worshipers. After a brief visit with the ushers and a few church members, Golden and Matthews left to worship at Central Methodist Church, a Black Methodist church welcoming everyone that day, Black and White.

But Golden and Mathews didn't leave quietly. They handed Rogers an open letter to the congregation, gently reminding them that "there cannot,

---

1. Cunningham, *Agony*, 55.

in fact, be any true Christian worship at all which is not intercession in behalf of all mankind, for Jesus Christ died and rose for *all*."[2]

Few scenes from the 1960s capture so well the deep and persistent divide in Methodism over race as this one. On one side, we have Methodists who continued to believe that the separation of races was divinely ordained; on the other, we have a growing body of Methodists who understood that integration and equal rights for Black persons were part and parcel of the gospel of Jesus Christ.

In this chapter, we'll take two related trajectories. We'll follow the MC as it moves from its segregated existence toward a more inclusive church. Then we'll trace the different ways Methodists resisted the civil rights movement.

The Methodist Church Struggles with Segregation

While the demolition of segregation in the 1950s and 1960s is often attributed to the various civil rights icons, it's essential to recall that the movement would never have gotten off the ground without the work of countless Black southerners. As one historian keenly observed, "Anybody that knows history, knows that when progress has been made, somebody behind the scene, unnamed, has made it all possible."[3] White Methodists were among the workers, but, by and large, the bulk of White Methodists, both laity and many clergy, were either silent or formed a persistent and ever-evolving resistance.

In this section, we'll follow the slow and, at times, tortured path of the General Conference where we begin to see a strong push against segregation, especially in the wake of the 1954 *Brown v. Board of Education* decision. But before we dive into the general church, let's take a brief look at where rank-and-file Methodists were on segregation. Fortunately for us, we can draw on the work of sociologist Dwight Culver, who studied segregation in the MC in 1953. While Culver did not sample lay people in his studies, he did reach out not only to pastors but also to district superintendents, whom Culver judged would tend to be more conservative than pastors, likely because of their position as custodians of the status quo.[4]

What did he find? Only slightly more than half of the White ministers surveyed agreed that "a nonsegregated church and a nonsegregated

2. Quoted in Cunningham, *Agony*, 58.
3. Curtis C. Bryant, quoted in Harvey, *Christianity and Race*, 153.
4. Culver, *Negro Segregation*, 19–41.

society" are Christian goals. About 25 percent completely rejected the idea. About half of the ministers who supported desegregation thought that fair treatment of Black persons was still possible under segregation. This meant that while many White pastors supported desegregation, they thought that segregation was not a problem for Black people. Almost 75 percent thought churches separated by race were fine for Black Methodists. Culver found that northern White pastors were generally more supportive of a church open to all races than their southern counterparts.

By contrast, Black Methodists surveyed were unanimous in opposing segregation in the church. While many White ministers believed that a racially segregated church offered Black ministers more opportunities, Black ministers said they were most interested in those opportunities that came through interracial work with White churches and White ministers.

Culver's work may lead us to think that there were just two groupings of Methodists during this period: integrationists and segregationists. We should also add into the mix a vast and often invisible middle group: moderate White Methodists, both northern and southern, who advocated for equal rights, but gradually. Bishop Marvin Franklin, who was elected to the episcopacy in 1948 and served the Mississippi Annual Conference, typified this view. He called for better schools and housing for Black families and urged White leaders to work toward "good feeling, better understanding, and finer cooperation" with the Black community to "live together and work out their common problems."[5] Even so, it seems fair to conclude from Culver's work that local churches, particularly in the South, were a long way from embracing integration.

Primarily because of organized resistance among southern Methodists, the denomination made slow progress toward bringing Methodists closer to that "beloved community" that Dr. King often spoke about. Those who planned GC1944 seemed completely unprepared for the reality of holding a joint, interracial conference in Kansas City, Missouri. Black delegates were housed in a separate part of the city, and their only source of food during Conference were the auditorium's snack stands. After nearly coming to a formal protest on the floor of Conference, arrangements were made to hire a local restaurateur to set up a dining hall at the Conference. One delegate reported that "the food was terrible, the service more so."[6] An official apology was offered up by the Council of Bishops, and a

5. Quoted in Reiff, *Conviction*, 18.
6. Quoted in Culver, *Negro Segregation*, 123–24.

resolution was proposed that future General Conferences provide food "without distinction on the basis of race." Emblematic of how hypersensitive this Conference was on race, even this was too much for some. The final amendment that was adopted recommended that "adequate and suitable entertainment" be provided for all delegates.[7]

Resolutions on race at GC1944 talked about segregation without using the actual word. "No group is inherently superior or inferior to any other, and none is above any other beloved of God."[8] The church remained committed to "the ultimate elimination of racial discrimination in The Methodist Church."[9] While a Conference Commission urged more robust measures, like more interracial meetings, an end to restrictive housing covenants, and a stronger minority ministry, they provided neither legislative nor budgetary proposals to make any of it happen.[10] Even forbidding segregation at national meetings, a recommendation from the Woman's Division, was shot down.

Succeeding General Conferences in 1948 and 1952 continued to press toward a church that stood for the equality of all persons, even calling into question the continued existence of the CJ. However, as historian Peter C. Murray notes, "The bishops did not specifically condemn *de jure* segregation as evil or call for the dismantling of the Central Jurisdiction."[11] In other words, Methodists were not able to move beyond egalitarian sentiments to the hard work of confessing and repairing the racist structure of the church.

We must note that the most passionate voices during this period in favor of the abolition of the CJ (and the end of segregation and discrimination throughout the church) came from none other than leaders in the CJ, like Charles Golden and James Brawley. In 1944 the CJ bishops offered a sharp critique: "We probably do not need to add a paragraph on the jurisdictional system which is one of those children's diseases which Methodism, if it is ever to become a healthy denomination, must outgrow."[12]

The 1954 *Brown* decision, which declared "separate but equal" schools unconstitutional, had the odd effect of energizing both sides of the church segregation debate. Just a half year after the ruling, the Council

7. Murray, *Crucible of Race*, 56.

8. Quoted in Culver, *Negro Segregation*, 14.

9. Richey et al., *American Methodism*, 180.

10. Reiff, *Conviction*, 17; Culver, *Negro Segregation*, 120.

11. Murray, *Crucible of Race*, 66.

12. Quoted in Thomas, *Dilemma*, 77.

of Bishops declared their support for the Supreme Court ruling, rooted in what they called a foundation stone of Methodist faith, "the belief that all men are brothers, equal in the sight of God."[13] Methodists outside of the South began more urgent conversations about eliminating the CJ. Meanwhile, over three hundred Methodists met in Birmingham, Alabama, to develop strategies to "maintain our current racial customs." Out of this meeting, the Association of Methodist Ministers and Laymen (AMML) was formed, soon to become one of the loudest Methodist voices advocating racial segregation and tying it closely to right-wing politics.[14] I'll say more about this group later in this chapter.

Several events point to a widening gap between youth and the church on matters of race. Methodist youth who were meeting in Indiana in 1955 challenged the church to move forward on desegregation. "We feel that the tragic fact of segregation is a serious detriment to the witness of the world Christian community."[15] In the 1950s, youth in the Southeastern Jurisdiction refused to swim in the lake at the Lake Junaluska Methodist encampment in North Carolina because, although Black youth delegates were present at the camps, they were not allowed to swim in the lake! A number of the state Methodist youth conferences were interracial and had to find alternate meeting places because White Methodist campuses would not welcome Black students.[16]

At GC1956, race relations and the CJ were at the top of the agenda, pushed along not only by the *Brown* decision but by other events, like the Montgomery bus boycott, which began in December 1955. At the Conference, as more and more discussions about the future of the CJ ensued, tempers flared just a bit. Bishop Oxnam, secretary to the Council of Bishops, remarked in his diary that "we made real progress although our southern friends are utterly impossible. . . . A generation has to die before we really reach a solution."[17]

The Conference made some progress on the status of the CJ, offering up Amendment IX, which would allow for the voluntary merger of White and Black annual conferences,[18] and it added to the church constitution a

13. Quoted in Hawkins, *Bible Told Them*, 33.

14. Dupont, *Mississippi Praying*, 131.

15. Quoted in Murray, *Crucible of Race*, 74.

16. Kirkpatrick, "Methodist Church," 28.

17. Quoted in Murray, *Crucible of Race*, 99.

18. Peter Murray observes that voluntarism was really a double standard, "since

commitment to end the CJ. However, since a merger could only happen if both conferences approved it by a two-thirds majority, it was a non-starter in southern conferences.

Reaction to Amendment IX was mixed. Southern Methodists were particularly enthused that the legislation was not forced, but voluntary, which they understood to mean that segregation in the church was the default.[19] The CJ, in a self-study, concluded that desegregation was complicated. While the segregated jurisdiction was immoral, it had created certain advantages for Black Methodists, especially in electing their own leaders and in representation on boards and agencies of the church. The report cautioned CJ churches not to jump headlong into White annual conferences believing that this alone would end racism in the church.[20] Historian Peter Murray points out that "African American Methodists were determined not to rush the process if it jeopardized their ultimate goal of a truly racially inclusive church."[21]

The delegates left GC1956 with a broad understanding that the CJ would be phased out but without any consensus about how and when that would happen. Various target years were bandied about, the most common being 1968. Not surprisingly, any date at all ruffled southern feathers. Many southern Methodists were under the impression that the 1939 Methodist union had made the CJ permanent. In South Carolina, the Board of Lay Activities announced that if separate jurisdictional conferences were to be "sacrificed upon the alter [sic] of integration" then many White churches would withdraw their membership.[22]

What was missing from the Methodist leadership was a simple declaration that segregation was an embarrassing evil, that it was a blight on the church's witness, and that the church would have much to gain as an interracial fellowship. Murray adds that there existed "a real fear of possible schism or mass defection" if leaders pushed too hard on integration.[23]

African American Methodists had not volunteered for the Central Jurisdiction." Murray, *Crucible of Race*, 114.

19. Years later, Lee Reiff, a Millsaps College professor, offered that "the Mississippi brand of voluntarism and gradualism means 'never.'" Reiff, *Conviction*, 234.

20. Richey et al., *American Methodism*, 181.

21. Murray, *Crucible of Race*, 102, 112.

22. Quoted in Hawkins, *Bible Told Them*, 108.

23. Murray, *Crucible of Race*, 102.

What happened to leaders who did push too hard? In 1955, after ten years living outside Mississippi, Roy Delamotte returned to take a pastoral appointment. At his annual conference meeting, Delamotte became more and more agitated that segregation was simply ignored. He knew pastors who disagreed with segregation, but none of them spoke up.

When a resolution from the annual conference to the upcoming GC1956 was being discussed, Delamotte could no longer be silent. The resolution called for the continuation of the current system of jurisdictions, including the CJ. He called for a protest vote against the resolution. The protest went down in flames, but the story didn't end there. The lay delegate at the church where Delamotte was to be appointed told the district superintendent they would not receive him as their new pastor. After long discussions that evening, the superintendent informed Delamotte the next day that no church in the conference would have him. The story of Delamotte's remarks at conference made the front page in local papers, much to the embarrassment of conference leaders, who seemed to value holding on to tradition in respectful silence. He was left with little choice but to transfer to another conference.[24]

In spite of the work of a four-year study commission, GC1960 failed to do much more than inch forward on racial justice. They did adopt a stronger position on race relations, mandated that every local church create a new Commission on Christian Social Concerns, and, along with Methodist women, created a quadrennial study on race for the entire church. They decided that it was essential to retain the jurisdictional system in the church but also, at some point, and preferably voluntarily, to abolish the CJ, effectively kicking that can down the road. Even with Amendment IX, the batting average for merging annual conferences after four years was exactly zero. The NAACP criticized the commission's report for its failure to end segregation.

In 1962, the CJ's study commission called for the termination of the CJ within a broader framework that would ultimately achieve "an inclusive Methodist Church." For the first time, the leaders of the CJ called the church racist, although it was changed to "racialism" in the report, perhaps to soften the impact. And they were quite clear that this hoped-for inclusiveness meant the empowerment of Black churches and pastors, not their isolation within a larger White institution. It meant serious attention and work on the

24. Reiff, *Conviction*, 21–22.

inequalities in income, facilities, and pensions. And finally, it would mean a serious transformation in the hearts and minds of White Methodists![25]

On the Path to Union and the End
of the Central Jurisdiction

In Pittsburgh, GC1964 assembled in the wake of an incredibly turbulent time. The nation had faced a presidential assassination, the March on Washington, the death of four young girls in a church bombing in Birmingham, and the forced integration of schools. Over a thousand youth from the Methodist Student Movement and Methodists for Church Renewal staged demonstrations at the General Conference by kneeling at the entrance to the arena, protesting continuing segregation in the church.

From the opening bell, it seemed clear that 1964 would be the year for the church to move forward. The Episcopal Address, given by Bishop Gerald Kennedy, was forthright in its rejection of segregation as somehow biblically justified and in its affirmation of the Methodist Church's open doors. Finally, the church was witnessing unequivocally to the absolute contradiction between segregation and the gospel!

The church's social justice stance widened considerably in 1964 to include, among other things, support for voting rights (including the pending civil rights bill), equal treatment under the law by law enforcement, open housing, and the right to protest violations of one's civil rights. The Conference created special funds that anticipated conference mergers, funds that would deal with financial inequalities (between White conferences and Black conferences) in ministerial salaries and pensions. In addition, they established a fund to assist pastors who had suffered because of their stance on civil rights, although since it was voluntary, it was poorly supported. The Methodist Church's new openness paralleled the national struggle to desegregate public facilities. The 1964 Civil Rights Act expanded the opening of all public places, such as restaurants, motels, hotels, parks, and theaters. It also created the Equal Employment Opportunity Commission, which enforced laws against racial discrimination.

In the fall of 1966, the General Conference met in Chicago for a special session to deal with two huge items: possible union with the Evangelical

25. Murray, *Crucible of Race*, 130–33. Meanwhile, southern White bishops reassured their congregants that "regional autonomy" would be preserved, code words meaning that there would be no forced integration!

United Brethren Church (EUB) and abolishing the CJ through something called the Omnibus Resolution. (Interestingly, the two issues were related, given that the EUB Church would not have joined the Methodist Church with the CJ still intact.) Prior to this Conference, church leaders had tried to end segregation in the church but to no avail. The heavy lifting would be left to this special Conference.

The Omnibus Resolution pledged "to do everything possible to bring about the elimination of any structural organization in The Methodist Church based on race at the earliest possible date and not later than the close of the Jurisdictional Conferences of 1972."[26] It also proposed the merging of the CJ conferences with their corresponding White annual conferences.

Opposition to the Omnibus Resolution was led by John C. Satterfield,[27] an active lay member in Mississippi, a commanding presence at General Conference, and a fierce opponent of the civil rights movement. Satterfield argued that there was not enough time for southern Methodists to fully digest the changes, and he recommended that the church continue voluntarism. In a refrain we have heard many times before, union of these conferences would only work when the hearts and minds of Methodists had changed. In his speech on the Conference floor, Satterfield added that if White and Black conferences were forced to merge, the church would lose at least a million members, a prophecy which, sadly, materialized over the next decade as Methodist attendance began to decline mainly in White but also in Black churches.[28] While membership decline cannot be blamed solely on race relations, that was certainly a leading factor.[29]

The Omnibus Resolution was approved by annual conferences and ultimately passed by GC1968, as was the EUB union. We would now be The United Methodist Church. And most important of all, after almost thirty years, the church was finally committed to eliminating its segregated jurisdiction. It was not immediately clear, though, whether the church could become truly inclusive, especially as racial divisiveness outside the church increased.

26. Quoted in Hawkins, *Bible Told Them*, 109.

27. In 1981, Satterfield visited with Bishop Minnick and confessed that though he had fought against integration, he was wrong and integration was working. Reiff, *Conviction*, 261. We should note that Satterfield was joined by other segregationists, including George Wallace, who was a delegate to GC1968 from Alabama.

28. Murray, *Crucible of Race*, 236.

29. Methodists were also divided over prayer in schools, the war in Vietnam, and feminism.

GC1968 set up salary and pension funds designed to ease the financial burdens of annual conferences as they merged together. The Conference also finally recognized that the shattered lives of those who lived in the inner cities—the riots, the unrest, the dismal housing—were a consequence of racism. As a result, $20 million was to be raised immediately for the new Fund for Reconciliation to address poverty and social injustice. One unique part of the fund was the United Methodist Volunteer Corps, created specifically for young people to work on local projects of reconstruction and reconciliation.

We can't leave this section without lifting up the formation of the Black Methodists for Church Renewal (BMCR). In response to the devastating riots of 1967, Black Methodist leaders met in Cincinnati in 1968 to form the BMCR. Black Methodist leader James Lawson, a pastor and civil rights activist, was deeply concerned the church was not serious about racial justice. On behalf of BMCR, he said, "We will settle for nothing less than a church where the love of Christ rules and where a man is a man not by race, or blood, but by the will and power of God."[30]

Lawson and the BMCR continued to challenge the church to step up its game, and the church responded by creating the Commission on Religion and Race. Its mandate was to hold the church accountable for dismantling racial discrimination and working with "prophetic movements for racial and social justice." That this was a huge step forward for the church was evident in the budget approved for the Commission; rather than the original $25,000, $750,000 was authorized for its work!

As part of the desegregation of the whole church, attention turned to the practices of Methodist institutions. We'll now examine how Methodist hospitals, colleges, and the Methodist Publishing House fared in this new world.

Desegregation and Methodist Institutions

South Carolina Methodist pastor James M. Copeland was not one to shy away from a fight. In 1959, he wrote a letter to the Charleston newspaper claiming that the vast majority of the MC was in favor of the "equality of races of all men" and opposed to segregation.[31] His letter reverberated like cannon fire throughout South Carolina, prompting heated responses in

---

30. Quoted in Richey et al., *American Methodism*, 202.
31. Quoted in Hawkins, *Bible Told Them*, 56.

newspapers across the state. On hearing that his response would not be published, Copeland wrote to the editor, "Segregationists really hate the light." Copeland was one of a growing group of younger White Methodists in the North and South who, following *Brown*, began to agitate for the desegregation of all Methodist institutions.

By the late 1940s, it's fair to generalize that most of the Methodist colleges and universities in the North were somewhat integrated, while few, if any, in the South were. Patients in Methodist hospitals were most often segregated by race. Of the forty-eight Methodist nursing schools, only nine admitted Black women. Of the sixty-seven homes (for children, the elderly, and "working girls") that reported back, only four had Black residents.

Over the next two decades, while those numbers improved slowly, the evidence of institutional racism was hard to miss. At the 1970 special session of the General Conference, the new Commission on Religion and Race reported on the state of Methodist homes and hospitals in relation to race. The makeup of the boards of these institutions was 99 percent White. Not surprisingly, most of those served were White and middle class. In response, the Commission called for stricter policies that would more closely reflect the new church's strong commitment to racial equality.[32]

GC1970 also received committee reports on hiring and employment practices in its agencies. One of the largest, the Methodist Publishing House (MPH), located in Nashville, Tennessee, was charged with failing dismally to live up to the church's social teachings. Barely one percent of the professional jobs were held by Black people. Almost 80 percent of the lowest-paid workers were Black. In one case, the committee found that in the mail room, in addition to unequal pay, new workers were hired from outside rather than promoting Black workers.

Apparently, this had been going on for a couple of decades. In the early 1950s, sociologist Dwight Culver recorded a conversation with the publishing agent and the editor in which they alleged that "the impossibility of hiring Negro secretarial help [was] supposed to be self-evident." The editor added that if he were to hire Black employees, they would be lonely, others wouldn't work efficiently, and, if there were more than one Black employee, "there would be trouble." Culver wrote that these discriminatory practices at the MPH were not generally known and were clearly in

32. Murray, *Crucible of Race*, 218.

complete disregard of policies the General Conference had adopted in 1944 and 1948 recommending "equal opportunity in employment."[33]

A further mark against the MPH was their failure to join Project Equality, a program created to push the adoption of fair employment practices for all churches and their vendors. James McGraw, a pastor in New York City, urged a boycott of the publisher until they joined Project Equality.[34] Under pressure, the MPH finally joined Project Equality, although in a lesser role as a supplier rather than as an active sponsor.

The 1968 investigative committee made several recommendations to end discrimination at the publishing house, including hiring a minority manager to promote job opportunities for minorities. For various bureaucratic reasons, the recommendations were not acted on until GC1972. By then, changes at the highest levels of leadership, affirmative action procedures, and more careful oversight of the MPH had wrought real progress.[35]

By the mid-1960s, many state colleges and universities in the South had been desegregated, at least in principle. Public schools were moving ahead more slowly on the same path, as were public parks, beaches, and accommodations. However, many church-related colleges and universities had yet to follow suit, and this arena became one of the next fronts in the war against desegregation. It's impossible to survey what happened at all of the Methodist colleges and universities, so we'll take up the story of one college emblematic of the kinds of struggles and decisions faced in other places: Wofford College in Spartanburg, South Carolina.[36]

The spark, in this case, was none other than James Copeland, who, at the 1962 South Carolina Annual Conference, moved that Wofford and Columbia Colleges "be open to all qualified students irrespective of race or national origin." After some debate, almost all of the delegates voted down Copeland's motion. In 1963, when Copeland brought his motion forward again, it was amended to read that the conference would place no constraints on the college trustees as they worked out their own policies on race. The amended resolution passed. Not a home run, to be sure, but at least a single on the path to desegregation at the Methodist schools!

The president of Wofford, Charles Marsh, informed the trustees that he had no personal objection to admitting qualified students, regardless of

33. Quoted in Culver, *Negro Segregation*, 120.

34. McGraw, "Practice What You Print."

35. Murray, *Crucible of Race*, 219, 225–26.

36. This discussion relies heavily on Hawkins, *Bible Told Them*, 86–93.

race, and saw strong ethical reasons for doing just that. But Marsh was also well aware of the opposition to such a move. In his statement, Marsh listed both the positive impact and adverse effects of a decision to desegregate. Of the various reasons he listed, the monetary fallout and the impact on recruiting faculty and students weighed most heavily.

In 1964, Marsh appointed a committee to study the desegregation of the college. Faculty were consulted in the process, and most responses were either grudging or outright acceptance of desegregation. The committee recommended that "no qualified student be barred from Wofford College on the account of race or creed."[37] Several months passed before the Board of Trustees voted to open wide the college doors.

The response to the Wofford decision was utterly predictable. Methodist churches in South Carolina and across the country angrily withdrew their monetary support in droves, which was not insubstantial. Fortunately, a shining knight came forward. Roger Milliken, a wealthy friend of the college, donated $1 million to help stabilize school finances, a welcome relief to Wofford's administrators.

Leaders at this Methodist school and so many others across the South sensed that the segregationist dam was breaking, and they could move policies slowly toward wide-open doors. Many of these schools functioned for a time as "White institutional spaces,"[38] a term coined by sociologists which meant that although the doors of the college were open to all, the institution, for all practical purposes, continued to function as a White space. The first Black students were admitted to Wofford beginning in 1964, and students recall those years as lonely and frightening. The worldview of segregation continued to exert its influence even in the face of desegregation.

The Theological Worldview of Segregation

As we work through these events and the resistance to Black equality, it's easy to conclude that southern White Methodists were somehow living contrary to their faith. Surely if you proclaim the universal "brotherhood" of humankind and love of neighbor, this would translate into an open church. In his book *The Bible Told Them So: How Southern Evangelicals Fought to Preserve White Supremacy*, J. Russell Hawkins argues that, on the contrary,

---

37. Quoted in Hawkins, *Bible Told Them*, 89.
38. Hawkins, *Bible Told Them*, 93.

"their faith *drove* their support of Jim Crow segregation."[39] In other words, southern White Methodist Christians were living out their faith as they understood it when they supported the separation of races.

What was that faith? Even though slavery had disappeared after the Civil War, the biblical and theological language that undergirded that awful institution remained. Segregation was understood, in many southern White Methodist churches, to be a manifestation of God's will. Rev. William Talley, a Methodist pastor in Florida, wrote that "birds, fish, and any animal you care to name is separated according to 'kind' in keeping with the primary creative formula by God Himself."[40] If one can learn about God through nature, through general revelation, then, so the argument goes, God must be a segregationist! To advocate for integration, then, was to contradict God's will. If that was not convincing enough, yet another argument was rallied forth: since the South had prospered (with the glaring exception of the Civil War!), this was a further sign that God was pleased with segregation.

Just as slavery had been defended by turning to the Bible, so was segregation. The Genesis story about Noah's curse of Ham and God's commands against intermarriage in the Old Testament were all recycled in support. Added to the mix was the story of the Tower of Babel, a favorite segregationist proof text. In Gen 11, we learn that "the whole earth was of one language and of one speech." The people migrated to a plain in Shinar and decided to build a city and a tower to make a name for themselves. Concerned about the scope of humanity's project, God stepped in and broke up the building party by confusing their language, "so they will not understand one another's speech" (Gen 11:7). Humanity was now separated and scattered across the face of the earth. For segregationists, the lesson was clear: southern apartheid was God's plan for the world and woe to anyone who endeavors to disrupt God's plans.

In a forum at Millsaps College in 1958, John Satterfield expounded on the biblical foundations of segregation. Satterfield, whom we've mentioned earlier, was a Methodist layperson from Alabama and a staunch opponent of the civil rights movement who actively worked to preserve segregation in the MC. In his talk, he quoted from Paul's sermon in Athens in the book of Acts, where the apostle says that "God has made of one blood all nations of men for to dwell on all the face of the earth and hath appointed . . . the

39. Hawkins, *Bible Told Them*, 4.

40. Quoted in Hawkins, *Bible Told Them*, 47.

bounds of their habitation"(17:26). This verse was cited most often by segregationists, who understood it to mean that God had fenced off different groups of people from each other, thus, supporting the segregation of races in the South.[41]

Efforts to "find" segregation in the Bible led to profound leaps of the interpretive imagination. One commentator claimed that Jesus was obviously a segregationist because, upon his return at the second coming, all the nations of the world would be gathered before him, and "he shall separate them one from another" (Matt 25:32).[42] Even as simple an interaction as that of Philip with the Ethiopian eunuch in the book of Acts was fair game; since they met together only briefly, this was a sign that the Spirit of God had preserved segregation (Acts 8:26–40). The examples are almost endless, and they found their way to laity through sermons, tracts, and Sunday school curriculum. Clearly, those who were fighting for integration and racial equality had their hands full, and, as a result, the desegregation of the MC would be slow in coming.

The Opposition to Integration Organizes

The White segregationist theology outlined here was not simply theoretical. It drove White church leaders into organized action to oppose integration in support of the existing racial hierarchy. Following the *Brown* decision, White Citizens' Councils popped up all over the South. The Councils were an organizational effort at the grassroots level to maintain the racial status quo and keep schools and communities segregated. The movement spread like wildfire across the South, boasting 250,000 members by 1956. Local church pastors, including Methodists, were heavily recruited and became a coveted windfall for the councils, adding not only a veneer of respectability but religious sanction to their work.[43]

Much of the success of the Citizens' Councils can be attributed to the intense economic pressure they placed on communities for support. Clergy who spoke out against the councils faced not only loss of financial support but public confrontations and grave personal threats.[44] The impact on the Black community was much direr. J. Russell Hawkins points out that if

41. Dupont, *Mississippi Praying*, 83–85.
42. Hawkins, *Bible Told Them*, 52.
43. Dupont, *Mississippi Praying*, 93.
44. Collins, *Church Bell*, 17.

Black parents tried to enroll their child in an all-White school, they "might suddenly find their credit cut off at a local grocery store or have their mortgage called in by the bank."[45]

When the South Carolina Annual Conference met in 1955, several Methodist pastors came concerned about the intimidation tactics of the Citizens' Councils. Two pastors, A. McKay Brabham Jr. and John V. Murray, authored a short statement, calling out the Citizens' Councils for pressuring citizens who were simply exercising their constitutional rights. The resolution was slipped into the docket toward the end of conference and, unexpectedly, it passed, although exactly how remained a point of contention.[46]

In a matter of days, the resolution and the pastors who wrote it came under heavy fire, even though it didn't mention segregation, nor did it explicitly condemn the Citizens' Councils. In the debates over segregation, subtlety was in short supply. Public opposition included the usual threats to withdraw support from the church and rousing endorsements for segregation. Murray was pastor of four small churches, each of which asked that he be relieved of his duties.

In theory, Methodist pastors were protected by the bishop and the long-held tradition of a free pulpit and, therefore, could not be dismissed by their local congregation. There were occasions when bishops did protect their pastors, but they were few and far between. After lamenting previous bishops in the Alabama-West Florida Conference, Donald Collins lauds the work of Kenneth Goodson. In his appointments and his support of pastors, Goodson "was committed to an open and just society both for today and tomorrow."[47]

In practice, however, amid explosive struggles over segregation, it became commonplace for laity to have an unpopular pastor transferred. In a move that seemed to some to reflect divine justice, Brabham moved out of the parish world to become editor of *The South Carolina Methodist Advocate*, where he would continue to be a thorn in the side of segregationists.

With the intensification of the Cold War in the 1950s and the Red Scare, some Methodists came under government scrutiny. In addition to individual Methodists whom it considered disloyal, the FBI flagged the Methodist Federation for Social Action (MFSA) and the Methodist Epworth League (which had not existed since 1939) as "tools" of the

45. Hawkins, *Bible Told Them*, 30.

46. For a fuller account of this story, see Hawkins, *Bible Told Them*, 33–39.

47. Quoted in Collins, *Church Bell*, 101.

Communist Party.[48] The MFSA was the oldest Methodist group organized for social justice and, especially, for fighting racism. It had already become a lightning rod for blistering attacks by conservative groups in the church. It was not long before the MFSA and several prominent Methodist leaders came under surveillance. The flood of conservative criticism against the MFSA came to a boil at GC1952, where the MFSA was officially prohibited from speaking for all Methodists. The MFSA went into a steep decline, and it was not until the 1960s and the civil rights movement that it began to flourish again.

Executive director of the MFSA Jack McMichael appeared before the House Committee on Un-American Activities (HUAC) in 1953 to defend the MC. In his testimony, he made constant reference to the teachings of Jesus and was finally asked by an exasperated committee member if he could leave Jesus out of the discussion! McMichael replied that he could not and that "in a situation like this, where guilt by association seems to be the principle on which you are operating . . . I am sure [Jesus] himself would long ago have been hauled before this committee!" Unfortunately, McMichael continued to be watched and harassed by the FBI long after the hearing. Bishop Oxnam also appeared before HUAC in 1953 and, in a remarkable testimony, exposed their shoddy investigative practices, their inaccurate reports, and what many perceived as violations of the separation of church and state. Oxnam's testimony was widely heralded and served to diminish the credibility of HUAC.[49]

One of the most combative of Methodist organizations opposing integration was the Mississippi Association of Methodist Ministers and Lay

48. Richey et al., *Methodist Experience*, 1:254–57.

49. Quoted in Richey, *Methodist Experience*, 1:255. In the wake of a host of social challenges at the end of the nineteenth century and the beginning of the twentieth—poverty, women's rights, racism, child labor, lack of unions, economic inequality, affordable housing—attention in many parts of the ecumenical church turned to the social implications of the gospel. For decades, Methodist pastor Frank Mason North led the church in social gospel initiatives, many of which intersected with racism, urging that the church had a key role in creating a more just society. North had a hand in founding the Methodist Federation for Social Service (MFSS, later called the Methodist Federation for Social Action or MFSA) in 1907 and in formulating the Social Creed the following year. The creed was strong on so many concerns in the social gospel movement, although a bit vague on issues of race, urging simply "equal rights and complete justice for all [people] in all stations of life." In addition to its advocacy work, the MFSA has continued over the decades to be a voice for progressive initiatives both in annual conferences and at the General Conference.

People (MAMML), formed in 1955.[50] MAMML was an outsized group, mainly composed of White laymen, whose influence reached far beyond their numbers. Well organized, MAMML fought for segregation on several fronts, sharing recruitment, mailing lists, and meeting places with White Citizens' Councils. MAMML battled against the Methodist denomination's social creed and the growing critique of segregation. Their criticism extended to bishops, annual conferences, and even to Sunday school materials![51]

In the late 1950s, a number of Mississippi Methodist churches petitioned the Methodist General Board of Education, claiming that educational materials, which sometimes pictured White and Black children playing together, were "integrationist propaganda"; in response, they declared that they would be boycotting Methodist literature.[52] Responding to the flood of discontent, which had begun in the 1940s, the Mississippi Methodist Conference filed a protest in 1960 with the General Conference, against what they called integrationist Methodist publications.[53]

In stark contrast to MAMML, there were other Methodist voices in this period. Carolyn Dupont notes that there were many moderates who were loyal to the MC and more open to political and social questions in the church. In Mississippi, as society became more aggressively closed, moderates began to speak out against segregationist doctrine.[54] In chapter 6, I'll lift up a number of these voices in greater detail, the impact they had on the church, and the consequences for those in the South who practiced prophetic speech.

The apparent impact of White resistance movements, which Methodist churches, leaders, and laity participated in, was to slow to a crawl any movement toward desegregation. The less public effect was even more devastating: the support these movements gave to the everyday violence and terror that Black people continued to endure.

Pastor C. W. Smith, who served a circuit of four churches in the early 1940s in rural Mississippi, was subject to constant harassment as he made his rounds. Underpaid, without cars, and easily picked out in their preaching suits, Black pastors in rural areas were common targets of White

50. A parallel opposition group formed in Alabama, the Association of Methodist Ministers and Laymen.

51. George, *One Mississippi*, 98.

52. Murray, *Crucible of Race*, 107.

53. Murray, *Crucible of Race*, 132.

54. Dupont, *Mississippi Praying*, 135.

hoodlums. In the conference records of the CJ, one finds story after story of violence faced by Black pastors and even by lay folks. Church services and conferences were often under police surveillance.[55]

Some bold witnesses in the South connected the dots between the aggressive work of segregationists and violence toward Black Americans. In 1962, in the wake of the riots that followed the integration of Ole Miss, Sam Ashmore, editor of *The Mississippi Methodist Advocate*, placed partial blame squarely on White Mississippi Methodists. It was an unusually bold statement from someone generally known for his even-handedness, particularly on issues of race. "Yes, the church is partly responsible for what happened at Ole Miss," Ashmore wrote, because they had not been "more vocal and outspoken."[56] The vast majority of White Methodists in the South, however, retreated into the proverbial cocoon of inaction and silence.

Questions for Discussion

1. What important steps regarding race were taken at the 1968 General Conference? Where were the failures? If you were old enough, do you remember that event and what your reactions were at the time?

2. When you read that, in the 1950s and 1960s, some Methodist leaders and organizations were flagged by the FBI as subversive and put under surveillance, how did that make you feel?

3. Do you think you would have risked speaking out for racial justice if you had been an active Methodist in these years?

4. How much responsibility for the failure of the church to integrate rests with bishops? What could bishops do today to address past failures?

55. George, *One Mississippi*, 85.
56. Quoted in Dupont, *Mississippi Praying*, 143.

6

Methodists and the Civil Rights Era (Part Two)

THEODORE PARKER, A UNITARIAN minister and an abolitionist, once said, "I do not pretend to understand the moral universe; the arc is a long one, my eye reaches but little ways. I cannot calculate the curve and complete the figure by the experience of sight; I can divine it by conscience. But from what I see I am sure it bends towards justice."[1] Dr. King reworked that thought into a phrase he used countless times, often crediting Parker: "The arc of the moral universe is long, but it bends toward justice."[2] In this chapter, although we will still see resistance, we will also find that long arc bending toward justice as more and more Methodists hear and respond to the call to end racism and White supremacy, both in the church and in society.

"Born of Conviction"

Early one January morning in 1963, Pastor Bill Lampton was confronted in his office by a local Citizens' Council member. "You've messed yourself up real good, boy," he warned. Lampton learned that church members planned to meet that evening and vote on his dismissal from Pisgah Methodist Church near McComb, Mississippi. The meeting never happened; congregations cannot vote to remove pastors, so the district superintendent had

1. Quoted in Worth, "Moral Arc," para. 17.
2. King, "Our God," para. 45.

called it off. The next evening, however, his car tires were slashed, and he was informed that if he didn't leave, there would be violence. Lampton and his family fled, and he never returned to that pulpit. He later clarified his exit: "It looked like I had another Ole Miss on my hands."[3]

The cause of this uproar? A statement published in the *Mississippi Christian Advocate* on January 2, 1963, entitled "Born of Conviction." Lampton and twenty-seven other young White native Mississippi Methodist pastors authored a manifesto written in response to the incredible silence from Methodist leaders over the riots at Ole Miss.

Their brief statement contained four affirmations. First, all Methodist pastors must have freedom in their pulpits to preach the gospel. Second, they supported the official teachings of the Methodist Church, which permit no discrimination "because of race, color, or creed." Third, they opposed the closing of public schools to subsidize private schools and committed to the church's support of the public school system. And, finally, they declared their "unflinching opposition to Communism," a tag integrationists were often labeled with.[4]

Reactions to the statement varied. Mississippi Bishop Marvin Franklin neither supported nor censured it. In the weeks that followed, the bishop and the district superintendents offered up this piece of milquetoast in their annual report: "Tensions of many kinds are in the world today, among them is that of race relations."[5]

The Mississippi Association of Methodist Ministers and Lay People (MAMML) strongly denounced the clergy statement, claiming that attacks on segregation were unchristian. In a preposterous case of misunderstanding, they somehow found support for their views in the writings of John Wesley, who, they argued, had rejected just this kind of ecclesiastical authoritarianism.[6]

Private support of the signers came from many directions and vastly outnumbered negative responses—college and seminary friends, former mentors, seminary professors, and Methodist church members mostly outside Mississippi. One of the most important public endorsements came from W. B. Selah, who pastored Galloway Memorial Methodist Church in

---

3. Quoted in Dupont, *Mississippi Praying*, 127 and Reiff, *Conviction*, 105–6.

4. See a copy of the statement in Reiff, *Conviction*, 289–91.

5. Quoted in Dupont, *Mississippi Praying*, 148.

6. Reiff, *Conviction*, 102.

Jackson, Mississippi, the largest Methodist congregation in the state. We'll return to Rev. Selah in the next section.

What happened to the courageous clergy who spoke out? There was a narrative at that time that if you spoke out against racism, especially in the deep South, you would be forced out of your church. This was certainly true for the majority of the signers, as it was for other clergy in southern Methodist conferences who spoke out.

At Oakland Heights Church in Meridian, Mississippi, even though the board voted down a motion to remove the pastor, many families left the church and contributions plummeted. Pastor Ed McRae made a routine hospital visit to a member, only to have her husband stop by the parsonage, blare his horn, and yell that he wanted nothing further to do with the church. When McRae asked him if he might talk over the matter like a southern gentleman, the man shouted, "You wouldn't make the pimple on a Southern gentleman's ass."[7] McRae left his church in June 1963 for the Southern California-Arizona Conference.

The "forced out" narrative, however, was not universal. Pastor Bufkin Oliver, who served in Ellisville, Mississippi, reported to an Ole Miss professor that his congregation had responded in "a splendid way" to his part in the "Born of Conviction" statement. He contemplated staying at his church, but, more out of concern for the safety of his wife and four children in the community, he moved to Arizona and eventually back to the North Mississippi Conference.[8]

All in all, eleven of the twenty-eight signers remained at their churches after the May 1963 annual conference, eight moved but stayed in Mississippi, and the others left for other annual conferences around the country. Eighteen months after the statement, twenty had left the state. The eight who stayed did so "out of a strong sense of commitment to the witness they had made," although the reasons for remaining were as various as the pastors themselves. Most found significant ways to stay active in seeking racial understanding and reconciliation, helping congregations weather the choppy waters of the 1964–65 civil rights legislation, assisting their local communities in complying with desegregation, garnering support for rebuilding Black churches burned in this period, and promoting economic development in impoverished communities.[9]

7. Quoted in Reiff, *Conviction*, 126–27.
8. Reiff, *Conviction*, 185.
9. Quoted in Reiff, *Conviction*, 198.

"Born of Conviction" was one of many clergy statements on race in this era. In 1954, the North Carolina Annual Conference passed a resolution supporting *Brown*. In 1957, following the crisis over the integration of Central High School in Little Rock, Arkansas, twenty-seven North Arkansas Methodist pastors joined a statement criticizing Governor Faubus, who had attempted to stop integration of the school.[10]

Like many of these primarily White Protestant clergy statements from the civil rights era, "Born of Conviction" was rather cautious. There was no general call for integration or the desegregation of schools. The civil rights movement and its goals and methods were left out, and the elephant in the Methodist room, the CJ and its elimination, was passed over.

Still and all, "Born of Conviction" was significant in its time. As historian Thomas Reiff argues, it came at a critical moment in early 1963, creating "a significant crack in the Closed Society's united front."[11] It served as a stimulus for dialogue about issues that White Christians in the South needed to discuss. Over against a theology closed to anything beyond the personal, the statement affirmed the legitimacy of the church's witness in a time of societal upheaval.

In 2013, upon the fiftieth anniversary of the "Born of Conviction" statement, the Mississippi Annual Conference Commission on Religion and Race honored the twenty-eight original signers with the Emma Elzy Award for contributing significantly to the improvement of race relations. Eight signers were present, along with their families. Myrlie Evers-Williams, the widow of Medgar Evers, also participated in the ceremony to honor and celebrate the courageous leadership of Medgar Evers fifty years after his assassination. This event was the first time the conference had recognized either Medgar Evers or the original signers of the statement.[12]

At this point, the reader may be wondering about the motivations of these twenty-eight clergy. Not why they signed the "Born of Conviction" statement, but as children of the South, where did the motivation come from to challenge the existing hierarchy? Some grew up in families that were more open-minded about race relations. But the golden thread running through almost every pastoral bio was two-fold: a seminary education that pushed them to see all human beings created equal and deserving of equal treatment and an unwavering commitment to returning to the South

10. Reiff, *Conviction*, 74.

11. Reiff, *Conviction*, xx.

12. Reiff, *Conviction*, 236–39.

and becoming part of its transformation. This may be their lasting legacy, teaching us to set aside our fears and welcome the new world God is ushering in right where we live.

Kneel-Ins

Every student of the civil rights movement knows about sit-ins. Among the first were those conducted in 1942 in Chicago organized by two Methodist graduate students, one Black, James Farmer, and one White, George House.[13] Few are aware of a movement that took place on Sunday mornings across the South beginning in the early 1960s. Instead of lunch counters and movie theaters, this struggle against segregation played out on the front steps of White churches, both Catholic and Protestant. In Jackson, Mississippi, for close to a year, civil rights activists, pastors, and church members engaged in direct, nonviolent actions to protest the blatant segregation policies of White churches. Typically, interracial groups arrived for worship at the church steps, hoping to break through the "color barrier." Most were turned away by a phalanx of ushers; some were arrested, even jailed.

The year 1963 was incredibly turbulent in the Magnolia State, with the beating and jailing of protestors, the murder of civil rights workers, and the burning and bombing of Black churches. One of the most violent sit-ins occurred at Woolworth's in Jackson in June. A year earlier, NAACP organizer Medgar Evers, along with a group of Tougaloo College professors and Black ministers, had organized a boycott of Jackson businesses to end racial discrimination.[14] Tougaloo is a historically Black college in Jackson, Mississippi. When the city turned down their demands, activists cranked up the heat, planning sit-ins at the Capitol Street Woolworth Store and pickets outside. While police and the FBI looked on, the demonstrators were attacked by a White mob. One student recalled that after some time passed sitting at the counter, "all hell broke loose. . . . The mob started smearing us with ketchup, mustard, sugar, pies, and everything on the counter."[15] They endured racial insults, obscenities, physical violence, and even had their skin burned with cigarettes. But they bravely refused to leave until the manager announced that the store was closed. As he left, his face bleeding and covered with restaurant condiments, Tougaloo professor John

13. Richey et al., *Methodist Experience*, 1st ed., 1:394.

14. Lyon, *Sanctuaries*, 42.

15. Quoted in Keating, "Agitation," 55.

Salter addressed the Jackson police captain: "Fine brand of Christianity you practice in Jackson."[16]

In the wake of the violence and intransigence of segregationists, Rev. Edwin King, Methodist chaplain and dean of students at Tougaloo, and Medgar Evers, NAACP field secretary, designed a new strategy. Perhaps the way into the hearts and minds of the segregationist powers in Jackson was through the churches. So began the church "kneel-in" campaigns, where interracial groups would approach churches, attempting to enter the sanctuary for worship. (They were dubbed kneel-ins because some of the groups that were turned away knelt and prayed outside the church before they left.) King, born and raised in Vicksburg and a graduate of Millsaps College, was highly active in the civil rights movement, continually challenging the church to "recover a more authentic Christianity."[17] He had the dubious honor of being the first White clergyperson to join the CJ, after being voted out of his home conference.[18]

Kneel-ins were designed, as King and Evers put it, to "bring the segregation issue to the conscience of white Christians"[19] and especially to those who might otherwise ignore it. While they fully expected to be turned away from the churches they visited, they hoped that their presence alone would spark debate and discussion within the church. The confrontation at the church doors was also designed to push the theological envelope and jump-start conversations. Were we reconciled to each other, Black and White, by Jesus or not? Was the church one or many? Was the MC committed to open communion and open doors or not?

On Sunday, June 9, 1963, the first kneel-in commenced. Evers escorted interracial teams, most of them Tougaloo students, to several downtown Jackson churches. One of the churches, Galloway Memorial Methodist, was home to the segregationist mayor of Jackson, Allen Thompson, and several leaders in the Jackson White Citizens' Council. Thompson and the city council had passed an ordinance earlier that year which made "disturbing divine worship" a punishable offense.[20] He had further instructed Jackson police that if a Black individual tried to worship in a White church, that

---

16. Quoted in Lyon, *Sanctuaries*, 54.

17. Quoted in Murray, *Crucible of Race*, 47.

18. Straker, "Non-Merging Streams," 110.

19. Quoted in Lyon, *Sanctuaries*, 60. Note that while I'm focusing attention on Jackson, kneel-ins were happening in other cities across the South.

20. Jones, *White Too Long*, 43.

qualified as a violation. Galloway was not initially a target for the teams; in fact, Evers had been led to believe that Galloway would open its doors to an interracial group.

After First Baptist Church turned away several students, they approached Galloway. Long-time Galloway senior pastor W. B. Selah had not only publicly supported the "Born of Conviction" statement, he had backed his associate minister, Jerry Furr, one of the signers. Selah, who was in favor of voluntary desegregation of public facilities and of the church, said, "There can be no color bar in a Christian Church."[21]

The ushers at Galloway turned away the Tougaloo students. While the service was underway, Furr told Selah what had happened outside. Selah delivered a shortened sermon on "The Spirit of Christ," and then announced his resignation, reading from a statement he had prepared weeks earlier for such a time. Furr also resigned.

The events of that first day—twelve Black worshipers turned away from four White Protestant churches and the resignations of two White Methodist pastors—garnered heavy press coverage. Selah received accolades from across the country, from Methodist clergy and laity, from missionaries and seminary professors, and even from members of his congregation, applauding him for his stand. One person wrote, "You have the support of many, some of whom are afraid to speak out, however."[22]

White Mississippi Methodists continued to defend their closed sanctuary doors with the now familiar cavil: that the church visit campaign was spearheaded by outside agitators who had no interest in worship at all. The two sides in this larger-than-life drama playing out on church door steps are aptly described by Carolyn Dupont: "A southern Christianity, in which a commitment to the racial hierarchy occupied a central place, and an emerging American version, in which an embrace of human equality was rapidly becoming a given."[23]

The week following the first church visits, Evers and King met to consider the way forward. Evers was moved by the courage of Selah and Furr, who had refused to minister in a church that practiced segregation. Tragically, this would be his last meeting. Later that evening, Medgar Evers was killed by a sniper in the driveway of his home.

21. Quoted in Lyon, *Sanctuaries*, 34.

22. Quoted in Dupont, *Mississippi Praying*, 153.

23. Dupont, *Mississippi Praying*, 165.

The church visit campaign continued into the fall, leaving chaos and confusion in its wake as churches and pastors wrestled over closed-door policies that not everyone in the churches had signed off on. One of the more bizarre juxtapositions in the campaign came on World Communion Sunday in October when churches typically focus on their unity with churches worldwide. Posters showing different colored hands receiving communion were printed on offering envelopes and church bulletins.

As families came to church that Sunday morning, they passed a much more substantial police presence replete with heavily armed officers, attack dogs, and police wagons. Three young women—two Black and one White—were arrested on World Communion Sunday as they tried to leave Capitol Street Methodist Church after being told they were not welcome there. The three were sentenced to a year in jail, and bail was set at $1,000, which was quickly furnished by two Methodist agencies, the Women's Division of Christian Service (WD) and the General Board of Christian Social Concerns. To put these arrests in context—the White men accused of bombing a church three weeks earlier had been fined $100 each and received three months in jail![24]

The arrest of the three women caught the public eye; it also proved to be a huge recruiting tool for the church visit campaign. As word spread across the country, waves of integrated groups descended on Jackson, prepared to go to church or to jail. Among the protestors was Jerry Forshey, pastor of Armitage Avenue Methodist Church, a mixed-race, inner-city church near Lincoln Park in Chicago. Several Methodist clergy in Chicago had formed the Inner City Methodist Ministers Fellowship, which worked on local issues of school integration, neighborhood change, and desegregation in their denomination. When Forshey and others read news about the three women, they began to mobilize groups of ministers (at the suggestion of Ed King) to join the kneel-ins.

Several pastors joined Forshey in creating Methodists for Church Renewal, formed to end the segregation of the MC. Forshey was the main organizer of the nine hundred or so protestors who demonstrated at GC1964 in Pittsburgh. They even brought a cross from Jackson, the very one that the KKK had burned on the grounds of Tougaloo College. The cross was later given to Forshey for his tireless work. Of the cross, Forshey said that it "was the gift of the Christ of shame, broken, and deserted and abandoned

24. Lyon, *Sanctuaries*, 115–16.

by his people and celebrated by those who also have participated in this brokenness."[25]

In November 1963, the Methodist Council of Bishops spoke directly to the problem: "The Methodist Church is an inclusive church . . . to arrest any persons attempting to worship is to us an outrage."[26] GC1964 approved the bishops' statement, but, as we noted earlier, failed to address the elephant in the room, namely, the continuing and shameful existence of the Central Jurisdiction.

It's difficult to assess the overall impact of the church visit campaign. As an effort to open up churches, the results were mixed. Months after the campaign started, while a few churches had opened to all, White Methodist churches remained closed to Black worshipers. And yet, the campaigns brought to visibility something that had remained hidden, and they forced White churchgoers to face the racial exclusion at the doorsteps of their own churches. The campaign did push GC1964 to pass a controversial resolution supporting civil disobedience. When facing laws that are "neither just nor valid as law," when all legal means have been exhausted, "the Christian conscience will obey God rather than man."[27]

As church doors gradually opened, sadly, many families who remained bitterly opposed to integration left for other churches. The campaign was divisive and painful, but clearly necessary if White supremacy were ever to be driven from the Methodist Church.

Headlights

Dr. King's famous "Letter from Birmingham Jail" was prompted by a letter from eight clergy, including two Methodist bishops, Paul Hardin and Nolan B. Harmon.[28] What sticks out like a sore thumb in their letter is how out of touch these church leaders were. They urged King and his supporters to continue working for their civil rights goals through the courts and negotiations with local leaders. How had they missed the news that the reason for direct nonviolent action was precisely because these avenues had failed? And how in the world could they even mention the "hatred and violence"

25. Quoted in Lyon, *Sanctuaries*, 252.

26. Quoted in Dupont, *Mississippi Praying*, 167.

27. Quoted in Collins, *Church Bell*, 96.

28. "Statement by Alabama Clergymen."

that direct action might provoke without naming the tsunami of violence devastating the Black community?

In his letter, King expressed his disappointment with the White church—with its complacency, its silence, and its irrelevance. King's eloquent characterization of the White church is both judgment and possibility: "So here we are moving toward the exit of the twentieth century with a religious community largely adjusted to the status quo, standing as a tail light behind other community agencies rather than a headlight leading men to higher levels of justice."[29] (King might well have added back-up lights to the list, for those who had resisted the great tide of justice.)

I'll highlight five Methodist individuals and groups who have been headlights for justice. As White Methodists, it's crucial that we see not only the truth of our past collusion with racism, but also see White Methodists who found the courage to push back against the torrent of racism. But first, we should emphasize that the MC had significant leadership in the civil rights movement: Black leadership! Joseph Lowery, a Methodist pastor, was cofounder of the Southern Christian Leadership Conference. Rosa Parks was a deaconess in the AME Church. Dorothy Height, who led the National Council of Negro Women, was one of six members on the core civil rights team. Civil rights leaders Gil Caldwell and James Lawson were also Methodist pastors.

1. From time to time, the Methodist Church did turn outward to tackle racism outside of its doors.[30] Growing national tensions over race pushed the WD and the Board of Christian Social Concerns of the Methodist Church to sponsor the Second Methodist Conference on Human Relations in 1963.[31] Over one thousand Methodists gathered in Chicago to discuss race relations. The mood was often contentious. A keynote address by Martin Luther King Jr. brought protests from some. The distribution at the conference of the letter that had prompted King's "Letter from Birmingham Jail" was vehemently challenged by one of its signers and conference attendees, Bishop Harmon.

---

29. King, "Letter." This sentence is omitted in some editions of the letter.

30. One innovative idea from Methodist communications was a national radio call-in show called "Night Call." The show, which debuted in 1966, featured dialog between Whites and Blacks. Guests included leaders like Eldridge Cleaver, Shirley Chisholm, and Stokely Carmichael. See "Night Call."

31. See Knotts, *Fellowship*, 245–47 for more on this conference.

Some of the most far-reaching recommendations on race relations came out of this conference. They called for the end of the CJ in 1968 and the elimination of discriminatory practices at all levels of the MC, including schools, colleges, and hospitals. Methodists were challenged to live in integrated neighborhoods and become more directly involved in the integration of public schools in their communities, voter registration, and desegregation of public accommodations. Many of these recommendations were passed on to and adopted by GC1964.

In 1964, as Congress debated the landmark civil rights bill that would have an enormous impact on desegregation, mainline churches lobbied in favor of the bill. The Methodist Board of Social Concerns directed Methodist leaders to engage in a letter writing campaign aimed at support of the bill; historians have recognized these actions as key to overcoming southern opposition.[32]

2. Some have charged that Methodist pastors who did not leave their segregated churches in the South sold out to the system. Certainly, some did. But many pastors who stayed continued to work for justice and equality, quietly and mostly unheralded. Donald Collins was a Methodist pastor in the Alabama and West-Florida Conference in the turbulent 1950s and 1960s. He offers a (White) insider view of the many ways the MC failed to respond to the civil rights struggle. But he also offers up numerous signs of hope, including the role of Methodist clergy in the integration of Auburn University.

In 1963, Harold Franklin, a Black graduate student, was denied admission to Auburn. A federal judge intervened and ordered the university to admit Franklin for the January 1964 term. To avoid a replay of the rioting and violence that had happened at Ole Miss, two Methodist ministers stepped in to help, Powers McLeod, pastor of Auburn First, and Maxwell Hale, Wesley Foundation Director at Auburn.

McLeod offered his office as a command center for the Justice Department and the FBI after Governor Wallace barred federal agents from coming on campus. They also procured housing for them when they discovered that Alabama State Troopers had booked all of the rooms the weekend Franklin was to enroll. Franklin and his attorney arrived at the church office before going to campus. There he was searched by FBI agents so that no one could accuse him of carrying a

32. Murray, *Crucible of Race*, 161–62.

concealed weapon. McLeod and a clergy friend drove behind the car that brought Franklin to campus, and he enrolled without incident.[33]

3. The Methodist Student Movement had a significant impact on the civil rights movement, encouraging students to take strong stands against racism, as well as against war and for gay rights.[34] One of the early volunteers in the first sit-ins in Birmingham in 1963 was a White college student, Martha "Marti" Turnipseed.[35] Her father, Andrew Turnipseed, a Methodist pastor, had become embroiled in a controversy over race back in the 1950s. He and other pastors in Mobile, Alabama, had signed a petition encouraging the city to de-segregate the city buses. Under pressure from segregationist laity in his church, the bishop was able to move Turnipseed to the New York Annual Conference.

On April 24, 1963, Marti Turnipseed joined seven Black students at a segregated lunch counter at Woolworth's in Birmingham. Later that day, she was arrested and expelled from Birmingham-Southern College.[36] She spent the next year at Millsaps but returned to Birmingham-Southern after they backed down on a requirement that she no longer engage in protest activities. Marti Turnipseed continued to offer her voice and witness against segregation in the church, including an impassioned speech to a huge crowd of over a thousand Methodists who gathered during GC1964. She urged delegates to end segregation in the church, arguing that if they didn't, not only Black Methodists in the South, but many White Methodists as well would feel abandoned.[37]

4. One argument often made in defense of good people who supported segregation, racism, and White supremacy is "that's just the way people were back then." Fortunately, that observation is countered by numerous examples of White people who grew up in a racist context yet overcame their acculturation, taking up the anti-racist cause amid powerful opposition. One was Florence Mars.

On June 21, 1964, three young civil rights workers were abducted and murdered by the Klan and law enforcement in Neshoba County,

33. Collins, *Church Bell*, 89–94.
34. Richey et al., *Methodist Experience*, 1st ed., 1:405.
35. Collins, *Church Bell*, 76–77.
36. Both Birmingham-Southern and Millsaps are Methodist colleges.
37. Lyon, *Sanctuaries*, 245–47.

Mississippi. They had been working on the Freedom Summer campaign, registering Black persons in Mississippi to vote. It was weeks before the bodies were discovered and decades before anyone was held accountable. Neshoba County was also home to Florence Mars, town matriarch and an active supporter of the civil rights movement. Mars famously said that in Neshoba County, "the basement of the past is not very deep," meaning that her neighbors still held on to antebellum notions of race and caste.

The Council of Federated Organizations (COFO), an umbrella civil rights group working on voting rights and desegregation, was active in Neshoba County. Mars was one of a tiny group of White Neshobans interested in their work. When she asked publicly why Black persons were discriminated against and mistreated, she was rewarded with a Klan-organized boycott and the end of her cattle business. If that were not enough, Mars was publicly humiliated by the local sheriff, who arrested her for drunk driving, a charge that, at that time, was unimaginable for a White woman. A year after the murders, Mars had hoped to speak to the youth at her church, First Methodist in Philadelphia, about what had really happened, but angry church parents asked the pastor to have her removed from the classroom, and Mars left the church.[38]

In her memoir of the 1964 murders, *Witness in Philadelphia*, Mars comments on the ironies and paradoxes of Mississippi—how the culture's openness and generosity were mixed together with a deep prejudice and hostility toward anyone challenging it. These paradoxes are also at the heart of this book as we continue to try to understand a culture that is steeped in the Bible and yet tolerates the most awful cruelties known to humanity.[39]

5. We can't let this section close without at least a nod to two of the most well-known Methodists of this period: Branch Rickey and Jackie Robinson. White baseball team owners enforced a strict separation between White and Black professional leagues, which ended when Rickey signed Jackie Robinson to the Brooklyn Dodgers in 1947.[40]

38. For a fuller account, see George, *One Mississippi*, 31–35.

39. George, *One Mississippi*, 34.

40. In the movie *42*, when asked about signing Robinson, Rickey responds: "Robinson's a Methodist. I'm a Methodist. God's a Methodist. We can't go wrong." There's no historical evidence that Rickey ever said that, but it does capture the importance of faith

While popular accounts of the integration of baseball focus on the main characters, Rickey and Robinson, the truth is more complex. Like so much of the civil rights movement, the integration of baseball was part of a huge social protest movement that began in the 1930s to demolish segregation in housing, employment, and other areas of life. In the case of baseball, it included the Black press, civil rights groups, radical politicians, White activists, and even the Communist Party.[41] The real story of Jackie Robinson is a continuing reminder that changes in systemic racism need more than larger-than-life characters; they require relentless grassroots movements of protest and activism.

Methodist Women Lead

Methodist women's organizations in the MEC had worked to change racial attitudes and eliminate systemic racism in the church and the nation. The range of their work during the civil rights era was simply astonishing. It seems there were Methodist women everywhere, whether it was lobbying for fair employment practices and voting rights or denouncing lynching and segregation, to name just a few. In this section, we'll only have space to touch on a few highlights. Recall that in the fondness of Methodism for constant reorganization and lengthy committee names, Methodist women were now members of the Woman's Division of Christian Service of the Board of Missions (WD).

The WD was exceedingly well prepared for civil rights work in this period. They had decades of interracial work behind them, and they were well-studied in biblical, ethical, and theological thought. The Social Creed, adopted by GC1908 and amended over the years, guided their work. The creed was unequivocal on human rights from the opening sentence: "The Methodist Episcopal Church stands for equal rights and complete justice for all men in all stations of life."[42]

Several women emerged in this period to provide crucial leadership not just in shaping religious teaching on civil rights but also in organizing and participating in work on the ground.[43] Thelma Stevens grew up

---

for both men.

41. Dreier, "Real Story."

42. "1908 Social Creed."

43. The scope of this book requires narrowing our focus to just two of many Methodist leaders. The list of significant leaders of Methodist women in the twentieth century

in Mississippi and committed her life early on to eradicating racism. She served as codirector of the Bethlehem Center in Augusta, Georgia, a busy community center where she developed some of the first interracial camping programs in the country.[44] Stevens led Methodist women from 1940 to 1968 as executive director of the Christian Social Relations and Local Church Activities (CSR/LCA). More than anyone, Stevens was responsible for educating Methodist women on the moral imperatives of the civil rights movement and how it was grounded in Scripture and in the teachings of Jesus. From there, women could be urged into work to change public policy.

Dorothy Tilly began her work by campaigning for improved educational opportunities for Black youth in her hometown, Atlanta. She worked with Jessie Daniel Ames against lynching, fearlessly traveling from county to county, confronting potential lynch mobs, or securing anti-lynching pledges from law officials. She urged Methodist women to sit in courtrooms as observers. Tilly once observed, "Justice would not only have to be blind, she would have to have a clothespin on her nose to stand what goes on in some of our courts all over the nation."[45] The presence of Methodist women in the courts brought about crucial changes in courtroom justice.[46]

Tilly became a friend of Eleanor Roosevelt's and served on President Truman's Civil Rights Committee, gathering overwhelming evidence of the harm done by racism and White supremacy. This experience was what tipped the scales for Tilly toward action on integration. She was active in every committee at the time having anything to do with race, including the WD, the CIC, the Association of Southern Women for the Prevention of Lynching (ASWPL), the Southern Regional Council (SRC), and the Fellowship of the Concerned which she founded. The Fellowship of the Concerned was an ecumenical and interracial group of churchwomen focused on working for justice in the courts, desegregation of schools, and voter registration. In the 1950s, Tilly endured accusations from her own church that she was a communist. At one point, the Klan threatened to bomb her home. Undeterred, Tilly considered this evidence that she was on the right track.

Women led the way in building a more inclusive church. In the 1940s, before the civil rights era, the CSR/LCA launched a series of national

---

would include not only Stevens and Tilly, but Carrie Parks Johnson, Cora Ratliff, Susie Jones, Theressa Hoover, and Peggy Billings.

44. Knotts, *Fellowship*, 104–7.

45. Quoted in Shankman, "Dorothy Tilly," 104.

46. Quoted in Richey et al., *Methodist Experience*, 1:203.

seminars held in the summers for Black and White women from the MC. One of the seminars explored the status and role of women in the church, a discussion that would begin shaping more just policies for the church in the near future. To achieve their goal of holding national meetings only where nonsegregated housing was available, all of the women at the 1956 conference in Washington, DC, stayed in a "Negro Hotel."[47] Thelma Stevens wrote, "This experience was good for many white women, some of whom protested vigorously. But it sounded an alert. Efforts toward more open housing in Washington were increased!"

Methodist women have always had a healthy inclination toward study, research, and education. One example is the fascinating connection between the WD and Pauli Murray, a lesbian feminist legal scholar and civil rights activist. The Woman's Division invited Murray to research segregation laws across the country. The project began as a pamphlet and quickly expanded into a book of 746 pages, the Methodist Women's equivalent of the *Green Book*! Was it legal to hold an interracial meeting in this restaurant or ride that bus together? Murray's book answered all of the questions. Methodist women not only underwrote the book but also helped place copies of it in six hundred colleges and universities and in every Methodist institution. The disturbing reach of segregation into every corner of life was a wake-up call for many.[48]

Their deep devotion to study also led the WD to write the first "Charter of Racial Policies" in 1952. The charter committed women to build a church and society "without racial barriers." And it laid out several practical policies for living out the ideal, such as hiring based on qualifications not on (White) race and holding programs where facilities were open to all people. The charter was renewed in 1962 and adopted by GC1964; it added, as an action item, challenging leaders to create more inclusive attitudes in their churches.

The first Methodists to respond publicly to *Brown v. Board of Education* were the Methodist women. At their general assembly in 1954, they adopted a resolution, rejoicing in the high court's decision and pledging to "work through church and community channels to speed the process of transition from segregated schools to a new pattern of justice and freedom."[49]

47. Quoted in Stevens, *Legacy*, 45.

48. Murray's book was also a key resource for the U.S. Supreme Court in the *Brown v. Board Education* decision. See Richey et al., *Methodist Experience*, 1:235–36.

49. Quoted in Knotts, *Fellowship*, 201.

The statement met with some resistance from southern delegates. Conference leaders framed it as aspirational, understanding that each community would have different approaches to racial justice. Although some southern conferences had threatened to rescind the charter, in the end no annual conference followed through.

In school districts across the country, Methodist women worked in small interracial groups to help integrate schools without incident. In Fleminsgburg, Kentucky, Methodist youth from the White Methodist church invited youth from the Black Methodist church for a Sunday evening meeting to help welcome them into the formerly all-White school. Methodist women helped make this happen.[50]

Methodist women hit early and hard on the desegregation of the MC. As they pondered the future of the CJ, these women took their cue from leaders of the Black caucus.[51] Their fundamental position was that the MC had lost the integrity of its witness because it was not truly racially inclusive. As they pushed toward desegregation of the church, they crafted a series of proposals designed to ameliorate inequalities between White and Black churches in resources, salaries, and pensions. They called for fair employment practices for the whole church and all its agencies, along with penalties for those who failed to follow through. They asked that mediation teams and funds be designated to meet the needs of the racial crisis in many American cities. They even recommended that the church provide bonds for folks who were jailed because they participated in kneel-ins. Many of these proposals were adopted at GC1964.

Although Methodist women had been studying race for decades, the denomination itself had provided scant leadership on race relations and civil rights. In response to the commitment of Methodist women to study race for four years, from 1960 to 1964, the entire MC would join them in a four-year study. Participants in the study were urged to do what many Methodist women had already been doing: form interracial workshops in their communities to help with desegregation, assist with voter registration, even engage with the civil rights movement and meet the leaders of nonviolent demonstrations. The WD, along with several other Methodist boards, set the example, joining the march for voting rights from Selma to Montgomery, Alabama.[52]

50. Knotts, *Fellowship*, 204.

51. Knotts, *Fellowship*, 240.

52. See the "Racial Justice Time Line."

Alice G. Knotts, in her comprehensive survey of the work of Methodist women on race from 1920 to 1968, is quick to point out that not all Methodist women were on board with every part of this work. A determined core group did the heavy lifting of dismantling racism. It's also important to remember that their work involved White and Black women working together each step of the way. Still and all, it's no exaggeration to say, as one historian put it, that the WD "mobilized Methodist women of all ethnic identities into one of the most sustained campaigns against racism ever witnessed in America."[53]

Conclusion

As we finish our overview of the MC in the civil rights era, several things come into sharper focus. First and most apparent is the painfully slow movement of the church toward *de jure* desegregation,[54] which wasn't fully realized until 1973 largely because the opposition inside the church itself was so formidable. The MC made some great strides forward: ending the CJ, creating the Fund for Reconciliation, and casting its support for the new voting and civil rights bills. But the ponderous move to desegregate the church against stiff opposition should put to rest any notion that the MC led the way in the civil rights movement. Of all institutions, the church was by far the last to desegregate!

Curiously, the Methodist leadership had little to no strategy in planning to move toward an integrated church. They could not have been unaware of the opposition they would face in the South and how opposition would strengthen when forced to integrate. Perhaps there was nothing that could have made a difference, but one wonders, especially in light of the work that southern women did, why some sort of pastoral strategy to "bring folks along" was not attempted.

When we talk about the integration of the MC, we need to be clear that, as many Black Methodists have taken pains to point out, desegregation and integration are not the same. Integration or inclusiveness is more than desegregation. As William McClain put it, *de facto* inclusiveness for the church is "the absence on all levels of church life of patterns and policies based on color."[55] McClain goes on to say that in the UMC, this has not

53. Richey et al., *Methodist Experience*, 1:235.

54. Many would argue that *de facto* segregation endures to this day.

55. Here McClain is quoting from the 1961 report *The Central Jurisdiction Speaks*.

occurred. Integration following the 1968 merger would essentially be on White terms, where White conferences absorbed Black conferences without having to make any substantial changes.

Several historians have observed that during this era, we find an organized opposition to desegregation undergirded by a theological framework that supported White supremacy. The central tenets of this "theology" are, first, a hyperfocus on personal morality over social justice, which means that systemic racism is invisible. The church's primary concern is with individual matters of piety and spirituality, not community issues like desegregation or civil rights. Second, a literalistic view of the Bible that is interpreted to support segregation. And third, a firm belief that racial change will only happen through individual spiritual transformation not political change. Most of the components of this "theology" do not disappear with desegregation but continue to vex the UMC.

Another theme that persists is the continued separation between the lofty pronouncements of the general church decrying racism and segregation and the actual practice in local churches. Robert P. Jones, in his book *White Too Long*, writes that during the civil rights era, "declarations on racial justice by national institutions and hierarchies were more often than not ignored or actively flouted by local clergy and their congregations."[56] The gap closes to some degree in the 1960s as we see more clergy and lay people, particularly Methodist women, vigorously working against segregation and racism. Although this is something of a break with older patterns of compromise and complicity with White supremacy, Methodists must still deal with the harsh reality that our church largely ignored the civil rights movement or forcefully opposed it.

Questions for Discussion

1. Were you surprised to learn that "kneel-ins" were used as a protest tool to combat segregation in churches? Where are you on the practice of direct nonviolent action to fight injustice when other efforts to change the system are not working?

2. How does the system of racial injustice actually produce a kind of indirect violence against Black people (for example, in the form of

---

McClain, *Black People*, 93.

56. Jones, *White Too Long*, 63.

poor health care and housing or discriminatory policing) that requires a response?

3. Do you agree with the statement that the UMC, in spite of changes in its structure and policies, did not really integrate? The author states, "Desegregation and integration are not the same. Integration or inclusiveness is more than desegregation."

4. How does our theological framework tend to work against direct action to end racism?

7

The Contemporary Struggle against
White Supremacy (Part One)

ONE OF THE COMMON myths about racism is that it ended in the U.S. with the civil rights movement, and that we now live in a post-racial society. That myth is easily shattered by a closer look at race relations. In this chapter, I'll survey race relations in the general church. Next I'll assess how we're doing on anti-racism work. Finally, I'll outline the shape resistance to anti-racism has taken.

The Larger Church

Following GC1968, the General Commission on Religion and Race (GCORR) was formed with Woodie White, a Black pastor from Detroit, as the general secretary. The commission was created to help the forthcoming merger of White and Black annual conferences, assist White Methodists in understanding systemic racism and the rise of Black power, and monitor the church on racial and ethnic inclusiveness. The unrest and chaos of that year, including the assassinations of both King and Kennedy, the continuing and sometimes violent demonstrations against the Vietnam War, and an election that revealed the deep divisions in the country surely added to the weight the commission felt in approaching their work.

One of their first challenges was responding to the Black Manifesto, a rousing proclamation by James Forman, which grew out of the National

Black Economic Development Conference (NBEDC) in Detroit in April 1969. Forman's presentation, delivered in the style of a jeremiad, lambasted White churches for their complicity in racism and demanded reparations, including "$500 million from Christian white churches and synagogues."[1] He made the manifesto public at Riverside Church in New York City in May 1969, dramatically interrupting the worship service to read it to the congregation, many of whom exited the church before he had finished. While most White Methodist leaders rejected the manifesto, some were able to set aside the revolutionary rhetoric and see the needed reparation work that was being called for. The Black Methodists for Church Renewal endorsed the Black Manifesto and campaigned for a reallocation of funds to support Methodist Historically Black Colleges and Universities (HBCUs).

On May 22, 1969, the four floors of the United Methodist Board of Missions offices in New York City were occupied for nine hours by a group organized by the BMCR with further demands. At their next meeting, no doubt influenced by the manifesto and the occupation, the Board approved several sizable grants totaling close to $2 million to the National Committee of Black Churchmen, the BMCR, the World Council of Churches Programme to Combat Racism, and the Methodist HBCUs.[2]

Methodism's continuing strife over racism was apparent at the special session of General Conference in 1970 in St. Louis. Black activists engaged the pre-conference meeting of bishops, and demonstrators were arrested outside Centenary UMC, the largest church in the city. The centerpiece of this Conference was a presentation by BMCR. Several hundred Black delegates and guests encircled the Conference floor. James Lawson, civil rights leader and Methodist minister, called for the church to work on reconciliation by focusing Methodist dollars on those most in need and allowing Black leaders to control the funds. The demands included heavily increased funding for inner cities, Methodist HBCUs, minority scholarships, as well as more representation of minorities in the boards and agencies of the church.[3]

GC1970 backed away from many requests, but they did reallocate $2 million not for BMCR but for the GCORR to use in assisting minority groups. They also authorized that the "Race Relations Sunday" designated offering be used for Methodist HBCUs. In the year prior, the offering

1. Forman, "Black Manifesto," 252.

2. Findlay, *Church People*, 201–5.

3. Murray, *Crucible of Race*, 216–17.

had only garnered $600,000, which would be a drop in the bucket when divvied up among all of those colleges and universities. In addition, they very nearly voted in an amendment to the constitution that would have allowed for quotas for minority representation on church boards and agencies. GC1970 seemed interested in equality; however, because of southern resistance, they could not achieve what former CJ leaders had repeatedly asked for, namely, equitable and meaningful representation in all areas of the church's leadership.

At GC1972, reports were received on the impact of the Fund for Reconciliation (which had been created in 1968 with a budget goal of $20 million). More than eight hundred projects had started up, many with the additional support of local government and private foundations. Black congregations were now administering outreach in a number of areas, including housing, drug treatment, youth services, prison reform, welfare, and health care. (By the way, that work has continued through the Minority Group Self-Determination Fund to the present day.) GC1972 also adopted the *Social Principles* in a revised form that strongly condemned racism and called for justice for all ethnic minority and oppressed groups.[4] And finally, mounting concerns about the pressing need for more work on racial justice led to the formation of a permanent Commission on Religion and Race.[5]

When the GCORR was first created in 1968, its primary purpose was to oversee the seemingly insurmountable task of merging formerly White and Black annual conferences in the South. A lay leader in Alabama confessed to Joseph Lowery the sad reality that the (White) North Alabama Conference would "sooner merge with Outer Mongolia" than with the (Black) Central Alabama Conference.[6] Some conferences merged without appointing any Black district superintendents. In some cases, the Black conference voted for the merger, and the White conference rejected it, prolonging the agony. When pressed for reasons, most White Methodists revealed with surprising honesty that they had not moved far on the continuum toward racial equality. Some White conferences approached the mergers with an old-fashioned paternalism, imagining that Black conferences would be joining the White conferences, rather than an actual melding of the two conferences into a new one, which was the intention of General Conference.

4. Richey et al., *American Methodism*, 205.
5. Murray, *Crucible of Race*, 226–27.
6. Quoted in Nicholas, *Go and Be Reconciled*, 283.

In South Carolina, for example, White delegates who voted against the plan for merger were deeply suspicious of racial quotas. They complained that the plan leaned too favorably toward the Black conference.[7] The BMCR saw it differently and had harsh words about the merger agreements: "White racism is accommodated and black people are negated and robbed of their humanity, integrity and dignity."[8] In spite of resistance, GC1972 set a July 1973 deadline, and all mergers were more or less completed by then. Without the tireless work of a new generation of pastors and lay leaders in the South, conference mergers might have dragged on forever.[9]

I won't go into this kind of detail for all the General Conferences up to the present day—that would take another whole book. The remainder of this section will be more like a highlight reel, taking note of special initiatives and attempting to get beneath the legislation to what was happening on the ground in churches as we slowly become a more anti-racist church.

In a clear effort to heal some of the damage caused by past racism, the general church expanded leadership by electing several talented Black leaders to the post of general secretary, including Randolph Nugent, Melvin G. Talbert, and George Outen.[10] In the decades that followed, the church encouraged the support of ethnic minorities, which included Black, Hispanic, Asian, and Native American churches and their leaders. By the late 70s, each group had its own caucus. This increased focus on other ethnic concerns, in addition to Black concerns, was crucially important, but it had the effect of dampening the work on anti-Black racism.

At GC1980, Methodists adopted the "Charter for Racial Justice" for the denomination. It committed local churches not only to addressing racist attitudes but also to exploring the impact of racism in their communities. The charter was brought to the Conference floor by the United Methodist Women (UMW), who had faced an earlier attempt to censure them over their alleged support of "terrorists" in Africa. In a moving defense of the UMW, none other than James Lawson cried out, "The women in the Women's Division are in our churches. If we are not where they are, we need to get ourselves where they are!"[11]

---

7. Quoted in Hawkins, *Bible Told Them*, 126–27.

8. Murray, *Crucible of Race*, 215.

9. See Nicholas, *Go and Be Reconciled*, for a full treatment of the painstaking work of Methodist leaders in Alabama toward merging.

10. A general secretary is the highest ranking staff person in a general agency.

11. "Racial Justice Backed."

The GCORR worked to equip the church to dismantle racism both inside and outside the church. In its dozens of workshops over several decades, the Commission helped White Methodists wrestle with White racism, White supremacy, institutional racism, integration, racial injustice, and color blindness. These workshops often led to changes in hiring practices, attention to affirmative action policies, and regular training on White racism at the general church level. Much of this work failed to reach pastors and local churches.[12] Methodists might be surprised to know that the anti-racism training they sign up for today has been going on in the church for almost fifty years!

One of the concerns raised by a deeper awareness of institutional racism was the need for open itinerancy, that is, the appointment of Methodist pastors to congregations without considering race. A parallel concern was that the salaries of Black pastors were not equitable. Since the 1968 union, Black pastors had raised concerns about their appointments solely to Black churches, describing it as a merry-go-round from one Black church to the next. Open itinerancy began to be addressed in workshops led by Woodie White and the GCORR in the late 1970s, at a time when it was virtually non-existent in the church.[13]

How effective was this work? While there are numerically more cross-racial/cross-cultural appointments being made in the UMC today, they have not reached the point of being simply the way Methodists do business. Jump ahead to 2020. Justin Coleman, a Black UM pastor, serves as Senior Pastor of University UMC, a White congregation in Chapel Hill, North Carolina. After he was appointed, he received congratulatory messages from across the country that he was in a cross-racial appointment. Coleman writes, " It pains me that we are still receiving calls like this in this part of the twenty-first century, but we know from the trauma of our society that we still have a very long way to go related to race relations outside and sadly inside the church." He adds, "I wish all United Methodist ministers thought of their appointments as antiracist appointments." Amen![14]

In 1987, the National United Methodist Convocation on Racism met in Louisville, Kentucky. Bishop Woodie White affirmed what we have already noted—that fighting racism in the Methodist Church was and still is

12. *Merger Review.*

13. White, "Open Pulpits."

14. Quoted in Rasmus, *I'm Black*, 83.

an "unfinished agenda."[15] A study done for the convocation revealed that while general boards and agencies had made strides on anti-racism, the issue has been largely ignored by annual conferences and local churches.

In May 1992, when Los Angeles erupted into violence following the acquittal of four police officers accused of the savage beating of Rodney King, General Conference was meeting in Louisville, Kentucky. The delegates took the unprecedented measure of stopping regular proceedings to discuss the events and how best the general church might act.[16] The response included a denomination-wide offering, a delegation to LA from GC1992, and the birthing of "Shalom Zones," which were designed to address the root causes of urban poverty and violence. The zones initially focused on immediate needs like housing, food, clothing, and water in a defined space in an inner city.[17] The Shalom Initiative continues today, although with a much looser connection to the UMC. Over the past thirty years, it has created hundreds of communities all over the world![18]

Throughout the 1990s, the GCORR continued working with annual conferences to recognize and respond to racist policies. But it also shifted gears just a bit to study racism in rural areas. The GCORR held hearings across the country and presented its findings to GC1996. Simply reading the testimony in the report raises the question of whether anything had changed in the church since the 1960s. The range of racial conflict in 1996 is simply astounding. A pastor cautioned against bringing Black children to Sunday School in a White Church. Taunts and barbs toward school children of color. Ethnic minority pastors struggling with low salaries and often without a parsonage. Cross burnings! Toxic waste dumped near ethnic minority housing. One theme across the board was how deeply hidden and embedded racism was in rural areas. A key part of the work of this task force was bringing racism and White supremacy out of hiding.[19]

Delegates to GC2000 participated in a worship service focused directly on the church's racist past. Called "Act of Repentance for Reconciliation," worshipers donned symbolic sackcloth and ashes, confessing to the sin of racism throughout the church's history and pledged to work for its elimination. The Conference adopted the "Act of Repentance for Racism," which

---

15. White, "Racism," 14.
16. Stovall, "Delegates," 1–2.
17. Bloom, "Practicing."
18. "Communities of Shalom."
19. "Racism in Rural Areas," 849–57.

called for education at all levels of the church about all forms of racism and encouraged annual conferences to hold "Act of Repentance" services, which many did.[20]

While the reconciliation service at GC2000 referenced the systemic racism that drove many Black Methodists from the MEC in the early nineteenth century, it made no mention of the racism Black Methodists endured who *stayed* in the MEC. At GC2004, in what may have been an attempt to fill in that gap, a special service of appreciation was held, "Celebrating Those Who Remained and Led the Way." Among those lifted up were Cecil Williams, pastor emeritus of Glide Memorial in San Francisco, and Leontine Kelly, the first Black woman elected bishop.[21] GC2004 also approved continuing the "Strengthening the Black Church for the 21st Century" initiative and creating the African American Methodist Heritage Center. The Center began in earnest, but unfortunately, much like the focus on racism, the budget diminished sharply over time.

By 2008, forty years since the dissolution of the CJ, Black Methodists were now five hundred thousand strong, with twenty-four hundred local churches and twelve bishops. The work and sacrifice of those who helped end the Black-segregated jurisdiction was honored at GC2008. Several speakers recounted how the CJ was both an instrument of Black empowerment and an ecclesiastical embarrassment. Angela Current Felder, a UMC executive staff member and daughter of Bishop Leontine Kelly, made the interesting observation that "without the memory of the Central Jurisdiction, we cannot know that it is possible to overcome a legacy of hatred and exclusion and move toward unity in Christ Jesus."[22] Surely these are words of hope for our continuing work on so many social issues!

GC2016 was forced to face the Black Lives Matter movement when church business ground to a halt as close to 150 laity and clergy marched onto the floor, surrounded the communion table, and chanted, "Black Lives Matter!" The group included members from various groups connected to the UMC, including the BMCR and the Reconciling Ministries Network. Pamela Lightsey, the first Black lesbian woman ordained in the UMC and a dean at Boston University School of Theology, helped organize the protest. She said, "We are upset about the lack of voice The UMC has given against police force (toward) black and brown bodies across the U.S. . . . which

20. Bloom, "Repentance Actions."
21. Green, "United Methodists."
22. Quoted in White, "Leaders Remember," para. 11.

says they do not intend to put the power of this huge denomination against this."[23] The UMC has yet to take a stance on Black Lives Matter. Meanwhile, Methodists have joined in Black Lives Matter protests and marches across the country,[24] and pastors and bishops are preaching on racial justice and policing from the pulpit.[25]

In the last decade, work on anti-racism has grown across the denomination. A quick internet search reveals dozens of trainings, study groups, workshops, conversations, and direct actions led by United Women in Faith (UWF, formerly the UMW), the GCORR, a host of annual conferences, and even some local churches.[26]

The North Texas Conference is one example of this growing anti-racist work. In January 2020, Bishop Mike McKee shared a vision for a new conference-wide initiative, "Journey Toward Racial Justice." At the conference level, they hired Ron Henderson, a Director of Diversity, Equity and Inclusion, who will have a seat on the bishop's cabinet. They've also just completed audits on racial equity that identify concerns such as understanding the unique needs of clergy of color and ethnic churches. Individual congregations were encouraged to take some kind of anti-racist action, for example, a book study, reaching out to a church of color, or doing implicit bias training. Nearly half of the churches in the conference have taken part so far. One key element in the initiative was the commitment of the bishop not only to encouraging anti-racist work but also "having the back" of pastors who might encounter resistance.[27]

In June 2020, the UMC Council of Bishops unveiled the latest anti-racist initiative: "Dismantling Racism: Pressing on to Freedom."[28] The website includes panel discussions on topics such as the theological roots of racism, voter suppression, how to be an ally, and White fragility. There are programs on implicit bias, how to move from book studies to anti-racist actions, how to create a Freedom School, and a thirty-day anti-racism spiritual practice. There's even a podcast, "The Unfinished Church," with

23. Quoted in Brodie, "Plenary Pauses," para. 5.

24. Patterson, "Smaller Communities."

25. Gilbert, "United Methodists Preach."

26. For a full list of what the UMC has said about racism, see the Baltimore-Washington Conference website, "2016 Social Principles."

27. This material was gathered from the website and an interview with Andy Lewis, Assistant to the Bishop of the North Texas Annual Conference of the UMC, December 5, 2022.

28. See "Racial Justice" for the initiative website.

interviews of activists and teachers, like Opal Lee, the "Grandmother of Juneteenth." And, happily, some of this work, especially in the area of individual anti-Black racism and prejudice, has filtered down to local churches.

United Methodist women have retained their historic laser focus on racial justice. In 1979, they founded the National Anti-Klan Network and adopted a resolution against redlining, a banking practice that effectively segregated cities by denying loans to prevent people of color from moving into certain neighborhoods. Recall that they brought the "Racial Charter for Justice"[29] to GC1980 for adoption. Since then, they've created Racial Justice Charter Support Teams to help resource churches as they respond to the call for racial justice in their communities. That work includes environmental racism, maternal mortality rates, the school-to-prison pipeline, and voting rights.[30] Over the last two decades, United Methodist women have engaged in resolutions, protests, public witness, and education on a wide range of issues from the criminalization of communities of color to the water crisis in Flint, Michigan.

Progress on Racial Justice?

So with all of this work going on, how are we doing on eradicating racism in the church? While there is little data on how Methodists are doing, there is helpful data on how White American Christians are faring on attitudes toward race. The Public Religion Research Institute (PRRI) and its founder, Robert P. Jones, have studied the relationship between White American Christians and White supremacy from several angles.[31] They have asked White Christians how they felt toward Black Americans on a scale where one is cold and one hundred is warm. White mainline and evangelical Protestants came out fairly warm, averaging scores between sixty-six and seventy-one—which is very close to the general public (sixty-seven). (United Methodists generally fall under either mainline or evangelical Protestants.)

However, when asked a different set of questions, say, on the impact of structural injustice and whether it is perceived as a barrier to Black upward mobility, the results are no longer so warm and fuzzy. In a 2018 survey, over 60 percent of White mainline Protestants and close to 70 percent of White

29. For the charter, see "Racial Justice," United Women in Faith.

30. Caviness, "Racial Justice Charter."

31. See Jones, *White Too Long*, 155–88, for a fuller discussion of the current relationship between White supremacy and the church.

evangelical Protestants disagreed with the statement that generations of slavery and Jim Crow created social conditions making it difficult for Black persons to rise out of the lower class. Black Protestants completely flipped on this, with almost 70 percent agreeing with the statement. It's difficult to imagine how Methodists can make much progress on eradicating racism if most White Methodists don't even see it!

Jones and his team have taken their research a step further. They have created a set of fifteen questions that together form a racism index. The questions are wide-ranging: "Attitudes about Confederate symbols; racial inequality and African American economic mobility; racial inequality and the treatment of African Americans in the criminal justice system; and the general perceptions of race, racism and racial discrimination."[32]

The scores range from zero to one, with zero reflecting the least racist attitude and one representing the most. The results are surprising and incredibly disappointing. White evangelical Protestants have the highest (or worst) score, 0.78. White mainline Protestants are not far behind, 0.69. This is glaringly above the scores of the general population, 0.57, White religiously unaffiliated Americans, 0.42, and Black Protestants, 0.24. Jones concludes, "White Christians think of themselves as people who hold warm feelings toward African Americans while simultaneously embracing a host of racist and racially resentful attitudes that are inconsistent with that assertion."[33] PRRI's quantitative evidence essentially confirms that White supremacy is still deeply ingrained in White Christianity and in the UMC.

Another way to assess our progress is to listen to persons of color. A recent book edited by Rudy Rasmus, *I'm Black. I'm Christian. I'm Methodist*, contains the personal faith stories of ten Black UM pastors. One of the central threads woven through these narratives is the unfortunate reality that racism in today's church is far from resolved. Erin Beasley, a pastor in Germantown, Tennessee, laments that "[we've] never dealt with our racist past." She is aware of the acts of repentance and the many apologies for past racism, but she argues that these efforts have not affected the local church.[34]

Vance Ross, Senior Pastor of Central UMC in Atlanta, agrees with Beasley. He writes that "there has never been a clear call to systemic change

---

32. Jones, *White Too Long*, 167.

33. Jones, *White Too Long*, 171.

34. Rasmus, *I'm Black*, 72.

that would be in the best interests of the Black church."[35] Ross brings some evidence to the table. He points out that Florida has only one Black church with more than two hundred in worship and "no United Methodist Black presence in Orlando, one of its largest and most populous cities."[36] In Philadelphia, San Francisco, Detroit, and Cincinnati, not one UM Black congregation has more than two hundred in worship. While this is anecdotal evidence, it certainly supports concerns that Black Methodist leaders and the GCORR have had for decades, namely, that in the wake of membership decline, the church has chosen church growth strategies that appear designed to grow White congregations to the neglect of Black congregations.[37]

Ross then goes on to enumerate how the UMC has failed Black churches in a whole host of ways. While Ross's disclosures go well beyond the scope of this book, they point to the need for investigation and reflection on the structures of United Methodism. And deep change![38] Here are just a few of the challenges he raises: the stripping of talented Black pastors from churches by offering higher salaries in connectional positions; assigning apportionments at the same percentage without accounting for the significant differences in Black and White income; selling unsustainable White church property to Black churches; and, essentially silencing the voices of Black people elected to general church boards and agencies.

Let's dig deeper into one example, the "stripping" of Black pastors from local churches to connectional positions for higher salaries. A recent twelve-year study undertaken by Duke University revealed that there are still vast disparities between the salaries of Black and White UMC pastors. This was a surprise to no one. The authors of the study, David Eagle and Collin Mueller, made several recommendations, including using apportionments to create more equitable salaries so that salaries are less connected to the size of the church.[39] Kenneth Carter, bishop of the Florida and Western North Carolina Conferences, confesses that the church often mirrors "the economic stratification of the culture, and this is certainly racialized."[40] This dramatic inequity in salaries between White and Black pastors is just one

35. Rasmus, *I'm Black*, 149.

36. Rasmus, *I'm Black*, 144.

37. "Racism in Rural Areas," 856.

38. Rasmus, *I'm Black*, 147–48.

39. Patterson, "Striving for Equity."

40, Patterson, "Striving for Equity," para. 16.

example of the many ways White supremacy continues to show its face in the contemporary Methodist church.

If this is not enough evidence that we White Methodists have a contemporary problem with the persistence of White supremacy, let's turn to two recent and rather public examples in the church. Chanda Innis Lee, who was born in Liberia and emigrated to the U.S. as a child, has been a UM pastor for ten years. She has been appointed in cross-racial and cross-cultural appointments, most recently at Fairlington UMC in Alexandria, Virginia. In an open letter sent to the United Methodist College of Bishops, Lee recounts "subtle and overt acts of racism and a plethora of microaggressions" in the church, "often to the detriment of our spiritual, emotional, mental, and physical wellbeing."[41] Ijeoma Oluo defines microaggressions as "small daily insults and indignities perpetrated against marginalized and oppressed people," either consciously or unconsciously, the cumulative effect of which does real harm and psychological damage.[42]

Lee offers four suggestions as part of her "Do No Harm" campaign, similar to what the GCORR has been demanding for decades.

1. Hold congregations publicly accountable for the harm inflicted on clergy of color by publicly sharing their stories as a call to repentance.

2. Require all cabinet members to take anti-racist and diversity training.

3. Require that local congregations who receive cross-racial-cross-cultural appointments take anti-racist and diversity training, and mandate that all congregations complete this work by 2024.

4. Create a staff position in each annual conference focusing on diversity, equity, and inclusion.

Lee hopes that her campaign will lead to transformation in racist attitudes in the UMC.[43]

The second example comes from the 2022 jurisdictional conferences where Methodist delegates across the church were electing bishops. The fact that this was one of the most diverse elections should be celebrated: more women and people of color were elected than ever before.[44] However, alongside the joys are concerns about the continuing stain of racism on the

41. Patterson, "Racism in the Ranks;" Lee, "Open Letter," para. 3.

42. Oluo, *Talk about Race*, 169.

43. Lee, "Open Letter," paras. 6–9.

44. Hahn et al., "Jurisdictions See Shift."

process. The Southeastern Jurisdiction will be forming a task force to study the impact of racial bias in the nomination and selection process for bishop candidates. As she withdrew from the election process, Rev. Sharon Austin, a Black candidate from the Florida Conference, warned that "we will never be the church we want to be when we treat people of color like they are commodities that can be easily discarded or used when we need photo ops, leadership and voices of color."[45]

Over the last fifty years, we have grown to embrace a deeper understanding of the meaning of White supremacy and developed practices to combat institutional racism. That these realities persist in our church means we have much soul-searching to do. And that work will be not so much a matter of the head, of acquiring more information—don't we have enough already?—but a matter of the heart, of the willingness to undergo the hard work of transformation for the sake of the kingdom of God.

The Move to Color Blindness

Throughout this book, we've tracked the different forms that opposition to racial equality has taken inside and outside of the church. Soon after its founding, the Methodist Church became complicit in racism through its support of slavery. When slavery ended, racism didn't end. Instead, it took the form of segregation backed up by Black codes and by terror in the Jim Crow era. The church followed suit, segregating conferences and meeting the terrors of this time with complacency and silence. We've noted that racism, while still very real, has become subtler over time and more challenging to weed out. Once segregation began to crumble, a new strategy developed. J. Russell Hawkins observes that "in the years after 1965, segregationist Christianity evolved and persisted in new forms that would become mainstays of southern White evangelicalism by the 1970s: color-blind individualism and a heightened focus on the family."[46]

We'll focus our attention here on the first form: color blindness. Color blindness is the notion that the best way to deal with racism is to treat everyone equally, without regard to race. You hear it openly expressed like this: "I don't see color" or "I don't care if you're pink, purple or polka-dotted."[47]

---

45. Hahn and Tanton, "Tackle Racism," para. 10.
46. Hawkins, *Bible Told Them*, 8.
47. DiAngelo, *White Fragility*, 77.

It may strike you as odd at first that color blindness is a problem. Isn't being color blind what we're all about? Don't we want to treat all people equally, especially in the church? Isn't this what Dr. King dreamed about in his rousing oration at the Lincoln Memorial in 1963, when he hoped one day to live in a nation where his children "will not be judged by the color of their skin but the content of their character"?[48]

Yes, yes, yes. All of this is true. But a critical distinction is missing. There's a huge difference between color blindness as the final destination of our anti-racism efforts and simply replacing anti-racist strategies with color blindness. Color blindness ignores how race and racism are embedded in history and in the various systems of our own time. A color blind approach dismisses the real-life experiences of people of color because race no longer matters. Also, color blindness is generally hyper-focused on individuals and racial reconciliation becomes all about building individual relationships. Suppose the ultimate solution to racism is that everyone is treated the same, irrespective of color. In a system that privileges Whites, this will work great for White people but will be disastrous for people of color.

In their study *Divided by Faith*, Emerson and Smith catalog the racialized patterns that are completely missed by the color blind approach. "It misses that whites can move to most any neighborhood, eat at most any restaurant, walk down most any street, or shop at most any store without having to worry or find out that they are not wanted, whereas African Americans often cannot. This perspective misses that white Americans can be almost certain that when stopped by the police, it has nothing to do with race, whereas African Americans cannot." Smith and Emerson go on to include several other systemic inequities that the color blind approach would miss: education, crime, wealth, income disparity, employment, and the judicial system.[49]

Color blindness appeals to White Christians because they no longer need to be concerned with racial inequality but with the perpetual attention to matters of race. In their minds, anti-racist work does not allow the wounds of racism to heal because it continually brings up race. Earlier, segregationists had used this tactic, often arguing that they were the ones who wanted to move into a future of equality by simply bypassing race altogether.

---

48. Quoted in Jones and Connelly, *Behind the Dream*, 117.

49. Emerson and Smith, *Divided by Faith*, 90.

Methodists in leadership should be familiar with this understanding of color blindness. In various "Workshops on Racism" led by the GCORR with all of the General Boards and Agencies, beginning as early as 1980, color blindness—a refusal to "see race as a part of [an] individual's identity"—is listed as an example of "personal and attitudinal racism."[50]

So how do well-meaning White American Methodists participate today in upholding systems of racism? One primary way is by latching on to color blindness. In every discussion of racism I've been a part of as a Methodist pastor, I've seen this color blind ideology at work. Our participation in it requires little energy. We stop talking about race, and White supremacy persists because we are unwilling to go to the root causes. Those opposed to anti-racism efforts, whether aware or unaware of their own color blindness, no longer need to rely on dated arguments from Scripture or the natural order about the separation of races. As historian Jemar Tisby points out, all the church needs to do today "is cooperate with already existing and unequal social systems"; in other words, do nothing, and our system will continue to benefit White people at the expense of Black people.[51]

So long as White American Methodists do not see racism at the level of structures and systems, our current inequalities and the harm they wreak will continue unabated. I like the metaphor Lutheran Pastor Lenny Duncan uses: "If we don't somehow find the moral courage to face systemic racism, name it as demonic, and have a proper exorcism, we will continue to be attacked by a legion of problems as we stumble into this already-bewildering century."[52]

Despite substantial resistance, the UMC has not given up on the struggle against the legacy of White supremacy. In the final chapter, we'll examine how several UM churches and leaders are working toward racial justice in their churches and communities.

Questions for Discussion

1. Based on your own personal experience, would you say that racism in the UMC has declined since the 1968 General Conference? How do you interpret the results of Robert Jones's statistical studies?

50. "Racism in Programs."
51. Tisby, *Color of Compromise*, 160, 171.
52. Duncan, *Dear Church*, 47.

2. What do you see as the benefits of open itinerancy? Would your church be open to a cross-racial or cross-cultural appointment? What needs to happen in the church for CR-CC appointments to work better?

3. How should the church address the income disparity between Black and White pastors and congregations in the interest of racial equity?

4. Do you agree with the author that color blindness is a problem in regard to race? Why or why not?

8

The Contemporary Struggle against
White Supremacy (Part Two)

ROBIN DIANGELO, A WHITE anti-racist educator, writes that the number one question that participants in her seminars ask her is, "What do I do?" While this seems like a perfectly logical request, DiAngelo finds it problematic. Her experience, over twenty-five years of teaching, is "that most white people don't really want to know what to do about racism if it will require anything of them that is inconvenient or uncomfortable."[1]

When we are willing to do something and begin to accept the harm-filled reality of systemic racism, several broad areas open up for churches striving to be more intentionally anti-racist. Many White Methodist churches, districts, and annual conferences have begun their anti-racism work with conferences and trainings that develop a deeper understanding of White privilege and how we White Methodists continue to engage in and uphold the system of White supremacy. Layla Saad's book *Me and White Supremacy* is a brilliant guide into this difficult personal work that is fundamental to shifting the culture of White supremacy and dismantling racism.[2]

Several authors have identified a number of racial justice practices that reflect an understanding of structural racism: pay reparations to Black people, remove Confederate monuments, learn from the Black church, host

1. DiAngelo, "Foreword," 2.

2. Other excellent resources to check out: *I'm Still Here: Black Dignity in a World Made for Whiteness* by Austin Channing Brown and *So You Want to Talk about Race* by Ijeoma Oluo.

a Freedom School, organize pilgrimages, fight for voter rights, publicly denounce racism, work for immigration reform and criminal justice reform (e.g., abolish the death penalty, overhaul police practices), and promote equitable public school funding. In the final part of this study, I'll focus on four areas where Methodist leaders and congregations are disrupting the architecture of White supremacy—Confederate memorials, the KKK and lynching, reparations, and policing policies. I hope these examples will illumine for all of us the hard but necessary work that lies ahead.

Symbols and Images

Let's return to 1980 and Union Presbyterian Seminary in Richmond, Virginia, one last time. Some dear friends had offered to drive me from my home in Toronto to Richmond. After checking in and unloading my gear, we hopped back in the car for a drive around the city. I'm sure we saw expansive parks and towering office buildings on our tour. To this day, though, what has stayed with me was the drive down Monument Avenue. I grew up around war memorials in Canada. But these Monument Avenue memorials were different. Perhaps it was my imagination, but the statues of Civil War generals seemed to be everywhere. (There actually are only a half dozen.) They were so large and set in such life-like poses that I half expected them to come to life, roaring into traffic to do battle.

But do battle for what? Here is where my limited understanding of American history let me down. I knew they were statues of military leaders, but what they had fought for and why they were so vividly memorialized on this beautiful tree-lined avenue escaped me. Looking back, I wish I had been just a bit more curious.

Robert P. Jones reminds us that Confederate monuments in Richmond had a close connection to churches. By 1930, seven of Richmond's leading churches had relocated to Monument Avenue, creating a sacred pilgrimage to the monuments themselves. Jones again: "As Confederate symbols were intentionally installed in prominent sacred spaces, where they were enmeshed with Christian symbols and justified by White Christian theology, they became religious weapons in the service of baptizing White supremacy."[3]

Since 1980, Monument Avenue has changed. Following the murder of George Floyd in May 2020 by a Minneapolis police officer, over 150 statues

3. Jones, *White Too Long*, 154.

have been removed across the country, including several on Monument Avenue. The Jefferson Davis monument was torn down from its pedestal by protestors. The Lee statue became a gathering point as artists transformed it by projecting images of George Floyd, Frederick Douglass, and John Lewis onto the base.[4] The last Confederate monument in Richmond was removed at the end of 2022.[5]

The history behind the creation of these monuments has become much clearer in our time. In her masterful study of Confederate monuments, Karen L. Cox concludes that they were created not simply to remember so-called Confederate heroes.[6] They were placed in prominent places to reinforce White supremacy and prop up White power over against movements for equality and justice for Black persons. The vast majority of these monuments were not erected as veterans' memorials in the aftermath of the Civil War. Most of them went up well after the war, with construction spiking from 1900 to 1930 and again in the mid-1950s through the 1960s. Recall that the early 1920s saw the rise of the KKK in a time of social and racial unrest. And the 1950s were essentially the starting point of the civil rights movement with *Brown v. Board of Education.* This is no coincidence. The periods of heavy monument construction during the Jim Crow years were reminders of who really held the power: White people.[7]

How have Methodists approached these memorials in their own communities amid the calls for their removal? While some Methodists advocate for removing these memorials, many others, particularly in the South, struggle with this out of loyalty to their Confederate ancestors. Although the UMC has not taken a position on Confederate memorials and their removal, several pastors and congregations have been called to this work. We'll look at four stories.

1. In the summer of 2019, two Charlottesville Methodist pastors, Isaac Collins and Phil Woodson, offered Bible studies at the base of the Robert E. Lee statue in Market Street Park, Charlottesville, Virginia. Dozens of people attended their early morning studies, "Swords into Plowshares: What the Bible says about Injustice, Idolatry and Repentance." Back in the summer of 2017, First UMC Charlottesville,

4. Cox, *No Common Ground,* 170.

5. Schneider, "Confederate Memorial."

6. Cox, *No Common Ground,* 14.

7. Jones, *White Too Long,* 119–22.

Woodson's church, had created a safe space during the deadly White nationalist march. People injured or traumatized during the march received medical treatment at the church. A young Black woman was surrounded by five elderly White women, who formed a protective human barricade for her as she left the church.[8]

The pastors have a unique take on the Lee statue. They hoped to drive home the point that the statues are idols created to bolster the religious underpinnings of White supremacy. In an interview, Collins said, "If you read the installation ceremonies, when they were put up, God is regularly invoked, there's religious vocabulary used about them, they're supposed to instill awe or reverence."[9] Removal of the statues, for Collins, does not erase history but removes idols and re-narrates a public space where real history can be shared. Woodson adds that churches can provide a witness to imagine a better future so that we're not passing along "the same systems of oppression and injustice."[10] According to Sally Hudson, a professor at the University of Virginia, this study in a public setting, pairing Scripture with a contemporary issue, seems to embody "the very best spirit of Methodist Christianity."[11]

Both the Robert E. Lee and Stonewall Jackson statues were removed in 2021, along with two other statues that celebrate violence against Native Americans.[12]

2. Sometimes, the Confederate memorial is in your own backyard. The statue of a Confederate soldier stands next to Mt. Zion UMC in Cornelius, North Carolina, where Jonathan and Angela Marlowe are co-pastors. According to the church's history, during the Civil War, the church served as an enlistment post for those who wanted to join the "Southern Cause." The land where the statue resides is private property and is not owned by the church. However, the local church history suggests that ties were closer after the statue was erected. Every year, beginning in 1900, a reunion of Confederate veterans took place

8. Lord, "Church Shelters Protestors."
9. Schneider, "Confederate Memorial," para. 4.
10. Bloom, "Seeing Removal," para. 32.
11. Natanson, "Confederate Monument Fans," para. 26.
12. "Charlottesville Removes."

on the church lawn, including a dinner, carnival rides, and a march to the tune of "Dixie."[13]

The pastors make the case that the continued presence of this statue violates John Wesley's first general rule, to do no harm. "Today, we are seeing very clearly the harm inflicted on Black people in our communities as a result of the long heritage of racism and White supremacy that pervade our society."[14] In July 2020, the administrative board of Mt. Zion together with the pastors called for the removal of the statue. In their statement, the board argued that the statue, which many perceive as offensive, is in direct conflict with their mission as a welcoming and hospitable congregation.[15] The North Carolina extended cabinet came out strongly in support of removing the monument. They rejected the argument that Confederate symbols are simply part of southern heritage, given that the symbols in question are constant reminders of a heritage of "shame, hate, intimidation and the degradation of a whole people."[16]

As of this writing, the statue remains next to church property with a sign stating that the monument and the land around it do not belong to the church. Marlowe says that the owners of the monument are uninterested in moving it, even though he has suggested finding a more appropriate location, like the church cemetery where Confederate soldiers are buried.[17]

3. In June 2020, three clergywomen were forcibly removed from the Tennessee State Capitol. UM pastors Neelley Hicks and Ingrid McIntyre were joined by their companion Jeannie Alexander in protesting the bust of Nathan Bedford Forrest housed in the State Capitol. Forrest was a Confederate officer and founder of the first iteration of the KKK following the Civil War. A proposal to remove the bust was voted down on the questionable grounds that the state didn't have the $3,500 to move and replace it.

Hicks and her colleagues watched the proceedings from the legislature balcony. After the vote, Hicks stood up and proclaimed that

13. Whisnant, *History*, 7.

14. Bloom, "Seeing Removal," para. 7.

15. The statement was sent in an email to the congregation. See "Statement from Administrative Board."

16. "Western North Carolina," para. 4.

17. Email from Jonathan Marlowe, September 14, 2022.

she had good news. "We have the $3,500 to move the statue." She was referring to money sitting in the state's rainy day fund, amounting to over $1 billion, which the state refused to use to remove the monument. She sat down and began to recite "The Lord's Prayer." When it became evident that the clergy were not leaving, state troopers were sent in to remove them.

Hicks left, but her colleagues stayed and had to be physically removed. Hicks emphasized that she was not advocating for the erasure of Tennessee history. She hoped the Forrest bust could be placed in a museum in the context of the state's racist history. As Hicks left the building, she had a message for the state troopers who escorted her: "This is sinful. This is wrong. God came to earth in a brown body. Forrest killed brown and black men. Your mama taught you better. Shame."[18]

In July 2021, the bust of Nathan Bedford Forrest was removed from its prominent place in the State Capitol. In a nod to the staying power of White supremacy, two other busts were also removed, both U.S. Admirals, apparently a compromise so that no one would think they were singling out Forrest. All three statues will be displayed in the Tennessee State Museum.[19]

4. Recent news that a UM church in Boise, Idaho, was removing a stained-glass window with the image of Robert E. Lee is a reminder that taking down Confederate memorials is not limited to the traditional South. The windows were installed in the Cathedral of the Rockies in 1960, allegedly promoting "a spirit of patriotism between white Northerners and Southerners." We've already noted that there was a spike in monument building in the 1960s as a White supremacist reaction to the budding civil rights movement that had nothing to do with hospitality. In response to the murder of George Floyd and the Black Lives Matter protests, previous efforts to remove the window took on new life.[20] Meetings were held and church leadership wrote to the congregation explaining the rationale for removing the window: "We recognize this section of our window is more than a benign historical marker. . . . For many of God's children, it is an obstacle to worship in a sacred space; for some, this and other Confederate memorials serve as lampposts

18. Astle, "Tennessee Clergy," para. 7.
19. Diaz, "Klan Leader."
20. Foy, "Boise Church," para. 13

along a path that leads back to racial subjugation and oppression."[21] The new window, installed in 2021, features Bishop Leontine Kelly, the first female Black bishop in the UMC.

What does removing a monument accomplish? Taking one down is not going to end racism. But advocating for their removal is a significant way of expressing solidarity with our Black neighbors and witnessing against them as continuing symbols of White supremacy. Perhaps the church could be a space for discussions about dismantling the Confederate symbols in our locales, especially given our history of either passively tolerating or actively promoting White supremacy.

Confronting the Klan and Lynching

Rather than face down the Klan and decry lynching, we know that numerous churches in the South and even in the North had connections with the Klan and White Citizens' Councils, providing members and leaders, even meeting spaces and monetary donations. As congregations now pursue their own racial histories, they often find segregationist skeletons in their closets or their communities. Here's what two congregations did.

1. In the late 1990s, Rev. John Flowers and Rev. Karen Vannoy, co-pastors of Travis Park UMC in San Antonio (1995 to 2005), caught wind of a story related to the church's chapel. Built in the late 1940s, the chapel was named after Marvin A. Childers, a prominent layperson in the church, a district judge, a regular delegate to General Conference, and a leader of the Judicial Council in the MC from 1948 to 1956.

    Judge Childers had also been a grand dragon in the Ku Klux Klan of the 1920s. Evidently, Travis Park had some prior history with the Klan. In 1922, when they hosted the Protestant Jubilee, Klan members in full White regalia marched down the aisle with a $100 offering and a letter of support for Protestantism.[22]

    When Flowers shared the news about Childers with the congregation, it jump-started a long overdue and challenging conversation about how a church can claim to be anti-racist but also have a chapel named after a beloved community figure who was a leader in the Klan. The leadership at Travis Park was divided on what to do with the

21. Banks, "Idaho Church," para. 3.
22. Learney and Galan, *Churches*, 74.

plaque and the name of the chapel. While many felt it was an affront to their faith and needed to be removed, some argued that the name should be preserved for the sake of history and out of respect for a significant lay leader in the church.

The board ultimately reached a compromise: not just the chapel plaque but all of the plaques in the church would be removed. Flowers kept the brass chapel plaque and took it to a metalsmith to have it melted down and then reformed into a communion chalice and paten. Both were presented to the St. Paul UMC congregation following a march from Travis Park to St. Paul that included pastors, leaders, and members from both congregations. St. Paul, a historically Black Methodist church, had been formed in 1866 as a church for newly freed enslaved persons from Paine Chapel MEC. Rev. Terrence Hayes, who pastored St. Paul from 1998 to 2004, recalled times of rich fellowship between both churches, something that rose above the history of racism and White supremacy out of which congregations like St. Paul were birthed.[23]

2. Along with many other United Methodist congregations, St. Luke's UMC in Indianapolis (SLUMC) was awakened into action by the televised murder of George Floyd on May 25, 2020. A predominantly White congregation, they had been working on racial justice for several years. But now the governing board decided that it was imperative for St. Luke's to make a stronger stand for racial justice. They revised their "Open Statement" to include specific language about becoming an anti-racist community, "pledging to be leaders in eradicating racism and discrimination."[24]

In the years that followed, St. Luke's staff and community developed a robust anti-racist program to engage folks where they are. Since May 2020, one hundred people have received anti-racist training, and one thousand have enrolled in anti-racist events. Their anti-racism work has transformed their internal hiring practices and their bidding process for building projects, making inclusivity a key value

23. Sources for this story include the following: the "Childers Statement," distributed by church leadership; an open letter to the congregation in the October 1999 issue of *Grace Notes*, the Travis Park UMC newsletter; and interviews with John and Karen Flowers, Byrd Bonner, Terrence Hayes, and Betty Curry (June-July, 2022).

24. "Who We Are."

in how they do business. They've also begun to explore what a more inclusive worship service might look like.

Beyond the church, St. Luke's annually brings together community resources for their annual "Northwest Incubator for Creators, Hustlers, and Entrepreneurs." This event focuses on resourcing minority-owned businesses that face all kinds of obstacles, particularly in financing and securing loans.[25] In addition, they host a Children's Defense Fund Freedom School which offers a six-week summer engagement program for children in under-resourced communities. Currently, they've begun work with the city on plans to provide a neighborhood resource center to be housed at the church.

Following a pilgrimage to the National Memorial for Peace and Justice in Montgomery, Alabama, the SLUMC racial justice team formed the Indiana Remembrance Coalition (IRC), which began investigating lynchings that happened in Indiana. With the help of a local history professor, the group gradually uncovered the lost story of George Tompkins, who was just nineteen years old when he was murdered in Indianapolis on March 16, 1922. His grave, in a local cemetery, is unmarked. The team discovered that Tompkins's hands had been tied behind his back, and his body tied by his neck to a tree. Coroners in the early twentieth century were reluctant to label the death of a Black man as a lynching, so Tompkins's death had been declared a suicide. This could not possibly have been a suicide. Of course, no one had been brought to justice.

Several church members working with a community group concluded it was a lynching and presented their findings to the county coroner. The death certificate was changed to "homicide." They also purchased a headstone for Tompkins and organized a memorial service on March 12, 2022, one hundred years after his violent death. Betty Brandt, a staff member at St. Luke's, said after the service that they wanted not only to memorialize Tompkins's life but also make the connection to racial violence today, particularly to the experiences of Black men with the police.[26]

The IRC began its work with the help of the EJI, which is committed to helping local communities "do the difficult work of unearthing

---

25. "Fair Housing Exhibit."

26. Sources for this story include: a phone interview with Betty Brandt (November, 2022) and an article by Leon Bates, "A Lynching in the Cold Springs Woods."

and confronting their own histories of racial injustice while exploring how that history continues to shape the present."[27] A number of
UM churches have worked with EJI to gather soil at lynching sites for
the Community Soil Collection Project[28] and to erect a marker that
describes the racial terrorism that happened at these sites. These are
tangible ways in which White Methodist churches can participate in
repairing the lies and telling the larger truth of our history.

Police Reform

The brutal televised murder of George Floyd in 2020 was a clarion call
for an end to police brutality and a drastic reform of police practices. In
June 2020, the United Methodist Bishops released a statement on racism
prompted not only by Floyd's murder but by the cascading series of deaths
of young Black men at the hands of police. The bishops affirmed that being
Black is both a gift from God and "a manifestation of God." They decried
the sins of racism and White supremacy and urged all Methodists to re-
claim their baptismal vows, standing against "the oppression and injustice
that is killing people of color." They urged Methodists to engage in deeper
education and in political advocacy.

The episcopal letter quoted Bishop LaTrelle Easterling: "The time is
now. Dismantle the architecture of whiteness and white supremacy; stop
creating, implementing and supporting policies that perpetuate economic
injustice; stop the dog-whistle political maneuverings which incite violence
against people of color; commit to being an antiracist; stop over-policing
Black and brown bodies; stop using deadly force in ordinary police interactions with Black and brown people. Stop killing us."[29]

This may be the strongest anti-racist statement to come out of the
UMC. While some would argue that these are simply words, they do have
an unparalleled force and direction. Past statements have typically relied
on general remarks about racism. In this one, the bishops confess to the
church's past silence and complicity and shout, "No more!" pointing toward
a future of action and, in particular, toward police reform.

27. "Community Remembrance," para. 3.

28. The Project gathers soil at the site of lynchings for display in a haunting exhibit
at the Peace and Justice Memorial Center in Montgomery, Alabama. See "Community
Remembrance," paras. 17–22.

29. "Scourge of Racism," para. 12.

The UMC Board of Church and Society has taken the bishops' call to address police reform one step further by providing a template for writing our elected officials. They urge several changes in police practices, including "establishing a national use of force standard, redefining police misconduct, banning chokeholds, banning profiling, and more."[30]

So are local United Methodist churches engaging in the call for police reform? Given that this is new territory for the church, the response has not been overwhelming. However, several churches have begun this work, and there are pastors for whom this is the center of their congregational racial justice program. We'll look more closely at three stories.

1. Former police officer and United Methodist pastor Shawn Moore has a unique approach to police reform. He now helps train police and believes that training in anti-racism, de-escalation, and cultural competency should be mandatory. He also believes that officers ought to carry out conversations and actions of reconciliation with the neighborhoods they serve. He points out that the first police in the USA were slave patrols and later officers who enforced the state terror of Jim Crow. Moore says, "For true reconciliation to happen in our communities, law enforcement has to apologize for acts in its history. The community needs to forgive and then ask what they can do."[31]

2. On June 27, 2022, in Akron, Ohio, police officers killed Wayland Walker following a traffic stop. According to the autopsy report, Walker was shot at dozens of times while fleeing police.[32] A group of fifteen United Methodist pastors in the area sent a letter to the city council calling for change in the attitudes and policies of local police. In addition, they urged the city to install dashcams in police cruisers and ban the use of tear gas, rubber bullets, and pepper spray in response to peaceful protests. The group of pastors has grown and continues the call for justice and change.

3. University UMC in Austin has had an active racial justice program for the past eight years. They work primarily in three areas—education of the congregation, monitoring of church practices, and advocacy in the community. One fairly consistent advocacy focus over the last five years has been their work toward changes in police oversight in

---

30. "Take Action," para. 5.

31. Hahn, "Pastors with a Badge," para. 36.

32. Cineas, "Deadly Police Shooting."

Austin. Civilian oversight of police would provide a crucial measure of accountability for the police department, particularly with violence against people of color.

The church's task force has taken on the mission of regularly attending negotiations between the city of Austin and the Austin Police Association, acting as citizen observers and pushing for accountability through civilian oversight. To get up to speed, they had to pursue research into complex city laws and procedures just to understand what was at stake in the meetings. Other than local media, the group from UUMC is the only regular group of citizens from a local church monitoring these negotiations. Following one session, members of the UUMC task force were invited to meet with the city attorneys and the chief contract negotiator to share their concerns. The group has also helped circulate and educate the congregation regarding a petition for a ballot initiative establishing an independent Office of Police Oversight.

I would be remiss if I did not mention that some racial justice advocates argue that police reforms alone are insufficient. For example, Philip V. Harris and Thenjiwe Harris, who advocate for the "Defund the Police" movement, contend that more training and diversity among police officers won't end police brutality.[33] Instead, they argue for defunding the police, which means, for example, reinvesting money spent on police toward alternative emergency response programs to work on emergency calls that involve substance abuse or mental health. While a discussion of the merits of this approach is beyond the scope of this book, some UM congregations will no doubt need to work with and understand defunding advocates if they engage in advocacy for police reform.

Working on police reform may seem far removed from the gospel. Given Jesus's concern for the health and healing of bodies, especially those on the margins, I would argue that it is front and center gospel work. Jemar Tisby puts it well: "Confronting the interlocking pattern of practices and policies that create and maintain racial inequality is what love looks like in public."[34] When we transform systems toward justice, we are indeed proclaiming the good news of the gospel.

33. McHarris and McHarris, "No More Money."
34. Tisby, How to Fight Racism, 180.

Reparations

Since 1996, the UMC has supported a resolution calling on Congress to adopt House Resolution 40, which would address the horrors of human slavery in our country and establish a commission to develop reparation proposals for Black Americans. Support for reparations is now in the latest version of the *Social Principles*.[35] In *The Book of Resolutions*, what is affirmed is "the discussion and study of reparations for African Americans" rooted not only in acknowledgment of the "massive human suffering" caused by slavery, segregation, and Jim Crow, but also in biblical texts, like Isa 61:1: "He has sent me to bind up the broken-hearted, to proclaim release to the captives."[36]

Given the limited scope of this book, I hope the reader will turn to other works, such as *From Here to Equality: Reparations for Black Americans in the Twenty-First Century*, by William A. Darity and A. Kirsten Mullen and *Reparations: A Christian Call for Repentance and Repair*, by Duke L. Kwon and Gregory Thompson, for a deeper dive into reparations. Darity and Mullen's work makes the case that, since the entire political order is complicit in the horrors of White supremacy, "the invoice for reparations must go to the nation's government."[37] Kwon and Thompson, while not disagreeing with this, make an equally compelling case for the church's role in reparations: "We call specifically the Christian church in America to embrace reparations as central to faithful Christian mission in this culture."[38] Especially given our long history of active complicity in undergirding White supremacy recounted in this book, how can we avoid an examination of our responsibility for reparations?

At this point, I'm sure some readers will want to push back. Surely the responsibility for reparations lies with the federal government. While I agree that the federal government has a moral obligation to engage in reparations, it's unclear whether this work will be taken up any time soon. This is where the church, whose mission is healing and repair, enters the picture. The church can be the moral voice for reparations and the moral actor modeling reparations.

35. See *Book of Discipline*, 120.

36. See *The Book of Resolutions of the United Methodist Church 2016*, 175–76. The *Book of Resolutions* collects all of the social policies and resolutions adopted by General Conference.

37. Darity and Mullen, *From Here to Equality*, 257.

38. Kwon and Thompson, *Reparations*, 210.

This proposal is not a new idea. Recall that decades ago, when James Forman proposed the "Black Manifesto," he assigned reparation payments to the church to the tune of $500 million! That assessment was rooted in many of the same uncomfortable truths we've uncovered in this book: that the White church helped enslave Black people, and that the White church benefitted from the forced subservience and exploitation of Black people.

So how is the UMC doing on reparations? It will come as no surprise that the church, like the culture, has resisted talk about reparations, which means that discussions of reparations are relatively new and actual reparation actions are few and far between. Interest in reparations seems to have grown over the last couple of years.[39] I'll lift up three White Methodist churches, hoping that their work will offer illumination and encouragement on this pathway for others.

1. One morning, I was reading the local Austin newspaper and was overjoyed to learn that First UMC Austin had repaid college debts for two hundred students from Huston-Tillotson University, a Methodist HBCU in East Austin. While they did not call their gift to the university reparations, it certainly walked and talked like reparations.[40]

   The gift grew out of a meeting of the leaders of both institutions, Taylor Fuerst, (White) Senior Pastor of FUMC, and Collette Burnette, (Black) President of HTU. FUMC has a long and rich relationship with HTU and has been active in racial justice work for years. Over time, they have acquired a deep understanding of the church's complicity and even practice of racial injustice.

   Dr. Burnette shared how COVID-19 had severely impacted a number of students, so Pastor Fuerst asked, "How could we help?" Burnette shared how financially challenged students were, especially with the pandemic, to the extent that some were in danger of dropping out. In response, leaders at FUMC planned their annual Advent and Christmas offering specifically for HTU students. The amount they raised was beyond their wildest dreams. Over $450,000, enough money not only to pay down the debt of students in crisis but also to create a fund for future students.

2. In 2019, the city of Evanston earmarked $10 million over ten years for reparations, with taxes from the sale of recreational cannabis as

39. Crary, "Racism-Linked Reparations."
40. Feldman, "Eliminates Debt."

the fund source. The city also committed to studying community recommendations for reparations. One of the first grants was reserved for housing grants for descendants of enslaved persons. Notably, Evanston is the first community on record since Reconstruction to pay reparations.

First UMC of Evanston, a primarily White church, has donated $50,000 to the city's reparation fund. Community activist Robin Rue Simmons is a former city council member and the driving force behind the reparations legislation. She spoke to FUMC about their gift, connecting the moral obligation to support reparations to the historical support of White supremacy in Evanston. "[FUMC] is leading by example," she said. "It is the white community who historically harmed the Black community, and it is the white community that has enjoyed privilege and access that the Black community has not. And so the white community has a responsibility and a role as an ally leader in the movement for reparations, and this church is modeling that with this important first step."[41]

The church's work began with conversations between the pastor, Grace Imathiu, Black, and Matt Johnson, White. Johnson, the church's lay leader, had been asked to serve on the stewardship committee at FUMC. He said he would serve under one condition: that they talk seriously about raising money around reparations. Led by Johnson, the church studied reparations during Lent and committed their special Easter offering to reparations.[42]

Contributing to the city's reparation fund is "not a big deal," Imathiu adds. "This is who we are. This is part of our DNA."[43] She's referring to a previous pastor, Dr. Ernest Tittle, who envisioned and prodded the church "to do justice to our fellow citizens of the Negro race, who rightly contend the question of social equality."[44] (Tittle was pastor of FUMC from 1919 to 1949.) Would that reparations and dismantling racism might become part of the whole UMC's DNA!

3. The final example comes from University UMC in Austin. I share it not because of its scope but as a creative way many congregations can

---

41. Patterson, "White Church," para. 8.

42. Interview with Matt Johnson, November 14, 2022.

43 Quoted in Patterson, "White Church," paras. 25, 26.

44 Quoted in Patterson, "White Church," para. 5.

engage in reparations. In our worship services, when we participate in congregational or choral singing, the composers are generally recompensed for their work. But what about when we sing "This Little Light of Mine" or "Swing Low, Sweet Chariot"? There are a number of African-American spirituals in our current hymnal—in fact, we have a special supplement devoted to them. But the names of the composers, if they were ever known, are forgotten. This history is a classic example of the theft perpetrated by White supremacy. In response, UUMC is following the lead of several churches around the country. As a compensation, every time a spiritual is sung in worship, the UUMC music program donates money to local Black music nonprofits as part of their commitment to racial justice.[45]

Why aren't Methodists more involved in reparations? I wonder if the root of our inactivity is what is at the center of this book. In order to consider reparations or take steps to undo racism, we must move out of the shadow of half-truths about who we are as Methodists into the full light of our complicated and complicit history. If we're not honest about the harm we've done, then what is there to repair? Kwon and Thompson remind us in their book on reparations that this work of historical confession is depressing, uncomfortable, even a bit humiliating work for most White people. But this is the only path to healing and repair: the path of humility.[46] As restorative economics practitioner Nwamaka Agbo frames it, "In order to bring about healing and wholeness we need to pause, reflect, and understand the patterns that got us here and then begin a place of having conscious choice about doing something different."[47]

Facing Our Own History Head-On

James Baldwin offered a salient observation on the crucial influence of history: "For history, as nearly no one seems to know, is not merely something to be read. And it does not refer merely, or even principally, to the past. On the contrary, the great force of history comes from the fact that we carry it

---

45. See LeMoult, "Some White Congregations," for a fuller account of musical reparations.

46. Kwon and Thompson, *Reparations*, 190–91.

47. Quoted in Kwon and Thompson, *Reparations*, 192.

within us, are unconsciously controlled by it in many ways, and history is literally present in all that we do."[48]

If we are serious as a church in working on racial justice, we must investigate our institutional histories and work toward repairing them. While we've done that on a fairly broad level in this book, we must also look at our own individual congregational histories. We must put our past dealings with race on the examination table and confess them before we can begin on the road to healing, transformation, and a more racially just future.

As I wrote this book, I attempted to practice what I've been preaching by exploring the racial history of the congregation where I served as senior pastor for eleven years, UUMC in Austin. The church has a local church history written in 1987 by Margaret C. Berry and Audray Bateman Randle. It seems most local church histories follow a traditional model of focusing on pastors, buildings, and mission programs, avoiding altogether controversial issues like race or war. There is no mention of the Central Jurisdiction, for example, of segregation or integration, of the Klan or White Citizens' Councils. In the 1960s, it's like the civil rights movement didn't happen. So I wasn't surprised to find no mention of the church's work in relation to race in our UUMC history.

UUMC, like many congregations, has preserved little of its primary source documents. Even without those documents, there are several things we can say about the racial past of UUMC with certainty. The church was founded in 1887 in the MECS, which means that we joined a denomination that historically supported slavery. From our study, we also know that the MECS supported segregation, was silent, or even supported Jim Crow laws, lynching, and the Klan.[49] The MECS was also the driving force behind the segregated CJ. Our local church histories must be rewritten to reflect these hard truths.

Edmund Heinsohn, who served University Church as Senior Pastor from 1934 to 1959, published his biography, *Fifty Years: Courtroom Pulpit*, in 1972, and he does not shy away from covering war and peace, nuclear arms, and race. At GC1944, Heinsohn spoke on the Conference floor ("as the grandson of a slave owner") in favor of the church's movement toward ending segregation. The local Austin paper got wind of this and published

---

48. Baldwin, "The White Man's Guilt," 47.

49. It's quite likely that there were University Methodist church members, even leaders, who were in the Austin Klan; it comprised about 10 percent of adult males in Austin in 1924. See Rambin, "Republic Square."

what Heinsohn had said. So Heinsohn went immediately to the University Methodist Board chair and asked how serious this was. The board chair replied that they all knew where Heinsohn stood, and while some disagreed with him, they were glad he had the courage to say what he did.[50]

In the mid-1950s, Heinsohn served as a member of the state advisory board on integration, and he applauded the move toward desegregation in the Austin schools and at the University of Texas. At GC1956, Heinsohn made a motion supporting the admission of members to the church "without reference to race, color or national origin."[51] That motion would be tested the very next year at University Methodist.

In the late fall of 1957, Heinsohn offered his year-end report to the official Board. With the University of Texas desegregating, Black Methodist students were seeking a church home while at school. University Church had opened its doors to Black worshipers and had received several Black students into membership that fall. When he concluded his report, a motion was made, "a vote of confidence," to support Heinsohn in opening the church to all. The Board stood unanimously in support of their senior pastor, although Heinsohn suggests this did not mean unanimous support for the policy itself. Perhaps in relief, he added a humorous anecdote. A layperson speaking with the church business manager complained that "the preacher has been preaching the kind of sermons that encourage this sort of thing [integration]." To which the business manager replied, "Yes, he has been preaching the gospel of love."[52]

Robert "Bob" Breihan served as campus minister to University of Texas students for twenty years beginning in 1960. While not directly connected with University Methodist Church, the campus ministry was right across the street from and often shared space with the church. Breihan drew students into the civil rights movement in Austin, working to integrate restaurants, movie theaters, and a newly opened skating rink.[53] While there was some church support for desegregation in Austin, the movement, in Breihan's words, "often rode on the back of students who put themselves at risk time and again through sit-ins and other nonviolent forms of demonstration."[54]

50. Heinsohn, *Fifty Years*, 203.
51. Heinsohn, *Fifty Years*, 206.
52. Heinsohn, *Fifty Years*, 217.
53. "Central Texans Reflect."
54. "Central Texans Reflect," para. 9; see also Buckley, "Desegregation."

Clearly, not everyone at University Church was on board with integration or Black equality, but, as we have seen so many times in our broader Methodist history, there was a nucleus of leaders who believed that fighting for racial justice was the work of the church. University Church's record on race relations has not been perfect, but it has risen above its racist beginnings in the MECS. Over the last twenty-five years, University Church has held a number of classes and workshops focused on seeing systemic racism, recognizing White privilege and supremacy, understanding the origins of racism in our country, and teaching children about race. The racial justice group I mentioned earlier was formed in 2014 to lead the church in study but also into the actual work of undoing racism in the church and community. A microlending team has done incredible work supporting local minority-owned businesses with zero interest loans. With justice work in its DNA, the leadership of UUMC is committed to building an anti-racist church. I look forward to seeing how far and how deep my church is willing to stretch into this work.

Conclusion

In this chapter, we've followed the UMC to higher ground as Methodists wend their way toward naming the sin of White supremacy and beginning the work that must be done to dismantle it. In the late 1960s, we offered training in understanding White supremacy, both at the level of individuals and larger systems. We created the GCORR to oversee training and to monitor how the church was doing on racial justice. Congregations, districts, and annual conferences slowly dipped into anti-racism work, even venturing beyond their walls into their communities. Even with all of this new work, ridding the UMC of White supremacy remains unfinished. If someone asks for evidence, we need look no further than the way Black pastors in cross-racial appointments are treated by their White parishioners, some of whose stories I've presented in this chapter.

Given that much of our racial justice work began more than fifty years ago, why do we have so little to show for it? Why does White supremacy persist in our churches? It is one of the most complicated and impervious systems humans have constructed. Over centuries, we have also built a formidable resistance to recognizing this insidious system. Pushing back against those massive systems is incredibly challenging. Layla Saad reminds those who take on anti-racism work that it "may sicken you and cause you to feel guilt, anger, and frustration."[55]

But here's the thing. White Methodists have an out. They can comfortably ignore racism and White supremacy without their lives being disrupted in any way. Even for church folks who long for an end to racism, there is a temptation to become what Rahkim Sabree calls a "conditional antiracist."[56] This is the notion that I will work on racial justice only so long as I don't have to change my quality of life and comfort. Sabree argues that, given enough pressure, the conditional anti-racist will "revert to conditions that mirror that of the racist bigot."

White Methodists can also fall back on color blindness, claiming that we are genuinely post-racial because we don't see color, and that those who do are the ones responsible for ongoing racism in our country. Which means that we return to a default where the table is tilted toward White people and away from Black people.

A similar complacency is true for the church at large. The UMC has never really acted with resolve to identify and tear down the hold of White supremacy on church systems and church people, particularly at the local church level. Lofty pronouncements, laments, and apologies are offered, but they have not translated into substantial budgets, staffing, programs, and long-term initiatives among local congregations. Like Las Vegas, what is said by General Conference stays at General Conference! Clearly, White supremacy has a longer shelf life than expected and will not be eliminated by simply making anti-racism an annual conference goal for 2023 or one of the quadrennial goals of GC2024.

Nevertheless, Methodists persist in the ways they always have. Small groups of clergy and laity in congregations across the denomination meet and work in areas that move beyond reading groups and anti-racism training. More often than not, United Methodist Women, now United Women of Faith, lead the charge. These United Methodists are turning away from silence and apathy toward engagement. They are opening up to a broader understanding of racism as an interpersonal problem and a systemic and structural problem. As a result, they are hosting Freedom Schools, offering minority-owned business loans, advocating for voting rights, lobbying for removing Confederate memorials, urging criminal justice reform, pushing for equitable public school funding, and even paying reparations.

55. Saad, *White Supremacy*, 13.
56. Sabree, "Racism," para. 7.

They're looking at their own hiring practices and also at the ways Whiteness has infected our theology and liturgy. In all of this, there is hope that Methodists are beginning to write a new chapter in race relations, one that understands that anti-racism is not a political movement but a requirement of following Jesus.

Questions for Discussion

1. What does removal of Confederate monuments accomplish? Where are the memorials—buildings, monuments, streets, schools, and so on—in your area?

2. Did you know about Methodist support of the KKK? Do you know about your church's history of involvement with the KKK? What do you think of the solution devised by Travis Park UMC after learning of their own history?

3. What do you think about the anti-racist actions taken by the churches described toward the end of the chapter? What actions do you think your congregation might be ready for?

4. How do you react to Rahkim Sabree's comment about conditional anti-racists? Now that you've finished this study, what will you do to dismantle White supremacy?

Conclusion

I CHOSE THE TITLE of this book, "Our Hearts Were Strangely Lukewarm," as a tip of the hat to our founder, John Wesley, the first Methodist anti-racist. As I hope you've seen in this study, the work of dismantling White supremacy has not been at the center of our church's work. Saying that our hearts have been "lukewarm" toward this work may be overly high praise. At times, we White Methodists have been ice-cold toward anti-racism, and warmed up toward simply preserving the status quo, which means maintaining White supremacy.

My ambition in writing this book is that our hearts will be opened up to a deeper understanding of our history and how we Methodists have acted as silent bystanders or even active accomplices in the enormous harm caused by racism. Given the many ways that White supremacy has bent and disfigured our own lives and the mission of our church, I hope that White Methodists will be roused to battle racism. Especially given how racism continues to produce profound inequalities, suffering, and violence in Black communities, I hope that our hearts will be stirred into action. Finally, I hope that the stories of Methodist folks who have stood against the tide of White supremacy and fought for equality, often at significant risk to themselves and their families, will inspire in us the courage that we can do this work as well. I can't imagine anything more important, especially in our time, than eradicating the plague of racism and White supremacy. I hope you agree.

So where do we go from here? My book is not a "how-to" on anti-racist work. Fortunately, there are excellent resources that cover that work quite well.[1] And yet surely, at the end of our study, it's worth asking what we

1. Here, I'm thinking of books like Joseph Barndt's *Becoming an Anti-Racist Church* and the plethora of resources at websites like gcorr.org.

can learn from our complicated history in dealing with racism and White supremacy. So here I offer not an exhaustive analysis but a preliminary list of eight actions I believe flow from this study. I present them not as one standing above the church in judgment but alongside the church, knowing that I have often struggled and failed to follow these rubrics in my ministry.

1. We must *restore the balance in the church between personal salvation and social salvation.* In our study, we've repeatedly found the church silent on racism or segregation because this was considered social or political work. The church was supposed to be about the salvation of souls. And yet we've also found the church has been quite noisy about alcohol, for example, and the temperance movement, which was most assuredly a public, political movement with a social impact. We can't have it both ways. We can no longer avoid uncomfortable issues we don't want to face by hiding behind the "spirituality of the church" and insisting that we must solely be about personal faith and individual salvation. We need only return to our founder, John Wesley, who clearly affirmed that our faith was both personal *and* social. If we accept that premise, then the church will always be both spiritual *and* political. *The Book of Discipline* puts it eloquently: "We proclaim no personal gospel that fails to express itself in relevant social concerns; we proclaim no social gospel that does not include the personal transformation of sinners."[2]

2. We must take this a step further and *restore the balance between mercy and justice.* Both mercy and justice move beyond personal spirituality. Mercy work is always more popular in the church. Justice work is avoided because it is a much harder to change systems and structures at the root of racism. And it can create tension because justice is perceived as partisan and political. Working at a breakfast for our unhoused friends (mercy) is much more fun and quite different than opening up our congregational practices to a racial equity audit of our employment and investment policies (justice). Mercy work has an important place in the full range of congregational outreach. However, substantial change will not happen without the kind of justice work that reveals and undoes the structural stranglehold of White supremacy on our church life. Advocacy for justice will be messy, difficult, even costly work. The generally accepted norm in many local

2. *Book of Discipline*, 55.

churches that justice work is somehow optional or that we can work on it at our convenience must end.

3. Restoring social justice to the church's ministry also means *recognizing the existence of systemic racism both in church and in society.* In their 2000 study of evangelicals and race in America, Christian Smith and Michael Emerson use the idea of a "cultural tool kit," a set of shared behaviors and ideas that allow people to organize reality in order to understand how people see racism. Missing from the White evangelical tool kit is any sense that social structures and institutions might shape social problems. According to Smith and Emerson, White evangelicals not only understand race issues as essentially interpersonal, but also "they often find structural explanations irrelevant or even wrongheaded."[3] Which means that we White American Methodists, who benefit from being White, don't see the system of White supremacy. If we are serious about dismantling racism in our churches and communities, we must begin by acknowledging the way White supremacy works as a system and its devastating impact on Black lives—for example, in wildly different health outcomes or in unequal access to quality education. Only when we see the built-in structures of racism in our culture will we know how to begin the work of healing and repairing.

4. We must *unmask our modern cultural myths about racism.* John Wesley exposed the myths and lies behind the contemporary defense of slavery and the enslaved trade. Let's follow suit. Let's lay bare the falsehood that racism and White supremacy were confined to the South. Let's call out the lie that racism is simply about personal behavior. In particular, let's tear down the fabrication that we live in a post-racial era and that color blindness will save us. Even though color blindness is not racist in itself, it can definitely aggravate racism because it refuses to see the reality of systemic racism and its pernicious impact on communities of color. As Michael Emerson and Christian Smith conclude, "A highly effective way to ensure the perpetuation of a racialized system is simply to deny its existence."[4]

5. We must *listen to the voices of our Black Methodist siblings.* This seems so elementary, yet our history suggests that we have repeatedly failed

3. Emerson and Smith, *Divided by Faith*, 78.
4. Emerson and Smith, *Divided by Faith*, 89–90.

to heed the concerns raised by Black Methodists. In the unions of 1939 and 1968, we failed to hear their lament about their continuing marginalization in a White-dominated church. What is not heard cannot be repaired. In her book on racial justice in Neshoba County, Mississippi, Carol George concludes that a critical factor in creating real change in the community was "for white Neshobans to take seriously the accounts of their black neighbors about injustice and mistreatment."[5] What are we not hearing today? I would suggest that, for one, we are not hearing the cry of our Black Methodist siblings that racism still exists at all levels of the church, especially the local church, and that White Methodist congregations must make an unequivocal commitment to the hard work of taking down racism at the interpersonal *and* institutional levels.

6. We must *restore the Wesleyan pattern of interpreting Scripture in conversation with tradition, experience, and reason.*[6] These four sources make up what has been called the Wesleyan quadrilateral, a guide to understanding our theology and our work in the world. The Methodist Church flew off the rails when it was guided by a simplistic, literalistic interpretation of Scripture. By falling back on a plain reading of Scripture, one which ignored historical circumstances and literary context, we found sacred authorization for the horrific system of chattel slavery, for the degradation of segregation and Jim Crow, and for a host of other evils visited on our Black neighbors. For that reason, we must be unafraid to look at the trajectory of Scripture, taken as a whole, which points toward a world where all humans are created by God and are of infinite worth.

7. It seems obvious, yet we must add this to the list: when faced with conflict, if we are to be faithful to the call of Jesus, the church must *choose truth over the preservation of institutional power.* At almost every turn, when the church was faced with choosing between proclaiming the truth and preserving the institution of the church (or the unity of the church, the size of the church, or the numerical impact of the church's witness), we chose the institution. John Archibald, whose father pastored Methodist churches in Alabama in the 1950s and 1960s, learned firsthand about the "conspiracy of silence" among

5. Dupont, *Mississippi Praying*, 232.
6. See "Our Theological Task," *Book of Discipline*, 80–88

Methodists. With rare exceptions, pastors, lay leaders, district superintendents, and bishops did not speak out on racial justice. Archibald writes, "Leaders of the church worried more about losing membership than they did about right and wrong."[7] Is it possible, however, that in siding with justice, the church might have opened itself more fully to new people, to segments of society that were vastly underrepresented in the church?

8. Finally, it should come as no surprise that *Methodist history needs to be rewritten and retold.* Methodists can and must dig beneath the veneer of respectability to uncover the truth about our past, much of which we have forgotten. We must tell stories where we have failed, compromised our most fundamental beliefs, and been unfaithful to the call of the gospel. After all, isn't the practice of confession fundamental to Christian faith?

We must also tell the stories of those few brave White Methodists who defied the system, like Gilbert Haven, Jessie Daniel Ames, Ed King, and Methodist women. And we must tell the courageous stories of so many Black Methodists who stood unflinchingly for equality, stories that span our history, from Harry Hosier and Richard Allen to Rosa Parks and James Lawson.

Where do we tell these stories? In church classrooms and worship services, on heritage Sundays and on bulletin boards, in seminars and potluck suppers. This truth-telling will have an enormous effect on church life. From the way we teach church history and theology, to the way we sing hymns and share liturgy in worship, all of it must be untangled from White European models that reinforce White supremacy. What would it look like for the UMC to take the lead on, say, a truth and reconciliation process for our denomination?

Our local church histories also must be rewritten. We need to ask questions and dig for answers about our church's relationship with race. When was your church founded? Where did they get the land, and who constructed the first buildings? Did the church move to a White neighborhood? Why? How welcoming has your church been, and how inclusive are your worship services, especially toward people of color? The path to repairing our relationship with our Black Methodist family must begin with a clear understanding of the very compromised history of our relationship.

7. Archibald, *Shaking*, 93.

Conclusion

Throughout our history, Methodists have reveled in high-flung pronouncements, overly ambitious programs, and soaring rhetoric calling for
justice. Over and again, we have said all the right things while doing little
or nothing in response, especially at the level of the local church. Given the
enormous and horrific burden of our racial history we drag with us, this
pattern, too, must change. We must choose a different path. Bishop Cynthia
Moore-Koikoi lays out the challenge: "The lives of my people and of all
people of color who've been systematically disrespected, disregarded and
extinguished by the sin of racism are too important to settle for anything
less than uncompromising *action* in dismantling racism. The same upris-
ing that has engulfed our communities must be unleashed in the church
interrupting business as usual until a breakthrough comes" (my italics).[8]
And that action must be more than the routine spasmodic protests that
we White American Methodists utter in response to a tragic event, like the
police shooting of a young Black man.

What gives me hope? This—even in the deepest gloom of racism and
White supremacy, the radiance of God's gracious power in the world was
never quite extinguished. We see it in the courageous rebellions of those
enslaved and in the formation of liberating Black churches. We see it in the
determination of those who decried the evils of slavery against all odds. We
see it in the resolve of those who stood against segregation and for equality,
bent on being anti-racist long before the word was used in everyday speech.
We see it in the courage of those who fought for equal rights at risk of life
and limb, intent on upending racism and White supremacy. It is finally in
their witness and in the irrepressible movement of God's Spirit that we can
find hope. May we join them not just in words but in deeds! And may we
find the strength to face our checkered past and move toward that horizon
of liberty, equality, and justice for all.

8. Moore-Koikoi et al., "Bishops Launch Dismantling Racism," para. 17.

Bibliography

(Note that several items marked GCAH are housed at the UM Archives and History Center at Drew University, NJ.)

"The 1908 Social Creed of the Methodist Episcopal Church." The General Board of Church and Society, n.d. Orig. pub. 1908. https://www.umcjustice.org/who-we-are/social-principles-and-resolutions/the-1908-social-creed-of-the-methodist-episcopal-church.

"2016 Social Principles and Resolutions on Racism." Baltimore-Washington Conference UMC, n.d. https://www.bwcumc.org/ministries/advocacy-action/racial-justice/2016-social-principles-and-resolutions-on-racism/.

Agnew, Brad. "Klan Was a Formidable Force in Methodist Church." *Tahlequah Daily Press*, Mar 10, 2015. https://www.tahlequahdailypress.com/news/klan-was-formidable-force-in-methodist-church/article_d84975b8-c72a-11e4-bf94-b71a9540be09.html.

Archibald, John. *Shaking the Gates of Hell: A Search for Family and Truth in the Wake of the Civil Rights Revolution*. New York: Alfred Knopf, 2021.

Astle, Cynthia B. "Tennessee Clergy Expelled from State Capitol in Statue Protest." *UM Insight*, Jul 18, 2020. https://um-insight.net/in-the-world/advocating-justice/tennessee-clergy-expelled-from-state-capitol-in-statue-prote/.

Baldwin, James. "The White Man's Guilt." *Ebony* (August 1965) 47–48. https://books.google.com/books?id=N94DAAAAMBAJ&printsec=frontcover&source=gbs_ge_summary_r&cad=0#v=onepage&q&f=false.

Banks, Adele. "Idaho Church Window Once Depicting Robert E. Lee Now Honors Black Female Bishop." *Church Leaders*, Dec 23, 2021. https://churchleaders.com/news/413347-idaho-church-window-once-depicting-robert-e-lee-now-honors-black-female-bishop.html.

Barber, Henry E. "The Association of Southern Women for the Prevention of Lynching, 1930–1942." *Phylon* 34 (1973) 378–89.

Barndt, Joseph. *Becoming an Anti-Racist Church: Journeying Toward Wholeness*. Minneapolis: Augsburg Fortress, 2011.

Bates, Leon. "A Lynching in Cold Springs Woods: The Sinister Case of George Tompkins." St. Luke's United Methodist Church, Jan 15, 2002. https://www.stlukesumc.com/article/a-lynching-in-the-cold-springs-woods-the-sinister-case-of-george-tompkins.

Bibliography

Beckford, Sheila M., and E. Michelle Ledder. *Anti-Racism 4Reals: Real Talk with Real Strategies in Real Time for Real Change*. Saint Louis: Chalice, 2022.

Bennett, James B. *Religion and the Rise of Jim Crow in New Orleans*. Princeton: Princeton University Press, 2005.

Berry, Margaret C., and Audray Bateman Randle. *University United Methodist Church 1887–1987: A Brief History*. Austin: Nortex, 1987.

Bloom, Linda. "Practicing 'Shalom' for 20 Years." *UM News*, Sep 11, 2012. https://www.umnews.org/en/news/practicing-shalom-for-20-years.

———. "Seeing Removal of Statues as 'Doing No Harm.'" *UM News*, Aug 10, 2020. https://www.umnews.org/en/news/seeing-removal-of-statues-as-doing-no-harm.

———. "United Methodists Continue 'Repentance Actions.'" *United Methodist News Service*, Feb 12, 2003. https://archives.gcah.org/bitstream/handle/10516/7700/article41.aspx.htm?sequence=1.

The Book of Discipline of the United Methodist Church 2016. Nashville: United Methodist Publishing House, 2016.

The Book of Resolutions of the United Methodist Church 2016. Nashville: United Methodist Publishing House, 2016.

"Boston Avenue United Methodist Church Justice and Reconciliation Initiative." Boston Avenue, n.d. https://www.bostonavenue.org/application/files/9716/2274/4817/Justice_and_Reconciliation_Initiative.pdf.

Brendlinger, Irv. "John Wesley and Slavery: Myth and Reality." *Faculty Publications—George Fox School of Theology* 41.1 (Spring 2006) 223–243. https://digitalcommons.georgefox.edu/ccs/116/.

———. *Social Justice through the Eyes of Wesley: John Wesley's Theological Challenge to Slavery*. Ontario: Joshua, 2006.

Brodie, Jessica. "GC2016 Plenary Pauses for Black Lives Matter Demonstration." *UM News*, May 16, 2016. https://www.umnews.org/en/news/GC2016-plenary-pauses-for-black-lives-matter-demonstration.

Brown, Austin Channing. *I'm Still Here: Black Dignity in a World Made for Whiteness*. New York: Convergent, 2018.

Bucke, Emory Stevens, et al. *The History of American Methodism in Three Volumes*. Nashville: Abingdon, 1964.

Buckley, Jordan. "The Desegregation of Austin's Movie Theaters." *Austin Chronicle*, Dec 4, 2015. https://www.austinchronicle.com/screens/2015-12-04/the-desegregation-of-austins-movie-theatres/.

Cameron, Richard M. *Methodism and Society in Historical Perspective*. Nashville: Abingdon, 1961.

Carey, Brycchan. "John Wesley's *Thoughts upon Slavery* and the Language of the Heart." *Bulletin of the John Rylands University Library of Manchester* 85.2–3 (2003) 269–84.

Caviness, Crystal. "Living the Racial Justice Charter." *UM Insight*, Sep 17, 2020. https://um-insight.net/in-the-world/advocating-justice/living-the-racial-justice-charter/.

"Charlottesville Removes Confederate Statues." Equal Justice Initiative, Aug 13, 2021. https://eji.org/news/charlottesville-removes-confederate-statues/.

"Charter for Racial Justice in an Independent Global Community." United Women of Faith, n.d. https://uwfaith.org/what-we-do/serve-and-advocate/racial-justice/.

"Chattel Slavery." Dictionary.com, n.d. https://www.dictionary.com/browse/chattel-slavery.

Cineas, Fabiola. "What We Know about the Deadly Police Shooting of Jayland Walker." *Vox*, Jul 7, 2022. https://www.vox.com/2022/7/7/23197430/jayland-walker-police-shooting-akron-ohio-footage.

Bibliography

Coates, Ta-Nehisi. *Between the World and Me*. New York: Spiegel & Grau, 2015.

Collins, Donald. *When the Church Bell Rang Racist: The Methodist Church and the Civil Rights Movement in Alabama*. Macon, GA: Mercer University Press, 1998.

"Communities of Shalom Initiative." United Methodists of Greater New Jersey, n.d. https://www.gnjumc.org/afwh/communities-of-hope/communities-of-shalom-initiative/.

"Community Remembrance Project." Equal Justice Initiative, n.d. https://eji.org/projects/community-remembrance-project/.

"Council of Bishops Statement on the Scourge of Racism." Council of Bishops, Jun 8, 2020. https://www.unitedmethodistbishops.org/files/websites/www/pdfs/cob+statement+on+racism+-+june+8+final.pdf.

Cox, Karen L. *No Common Ground: Confederate Monuments and the Ongoing Fight for Racial Justice*. Chapel Hill: University of North Carolina Press, 2021.

Crary, David. "More U.S. Churches Are Committing to Racism-Linked Reparations." *PBS*, Dec 13, 2020. https://www.pbs.org/newshour/nation/more-us-churches-are-committing-to-racism-linked-reparations.

Culver, Dwight W. *Negro Segregation in the Methodist Church*. New Haven: Yale University Press, 1953.

Cunningham, W. J. *Agony at Galloway: One Church's Struggle with Social Change*. Jackson: University Press of Mississippi, 1980.

Darity, William A., and Kirsten A. Mullen. *From Here to Equality: Reparations for Black Americans in the Twenty-First Century*. Chapel Hill: University of North Carolina Press, 2020.

Davis, David Brion. *Inhuman Bondage: The Rise and Fall of Slavery in the New World*. Oxford: Oxford University Press, 2006.

Davis, Morris L. *The Methodist Unification: Christianity and the Politics of Race in the Jim Crow Era*. New York: New York University Press, 2008.

Dearstyne, Bruce W. *The Spirit of New York: Defining Events in the Empire State's History*. Albany: State University of New York Press, 2015.

DiAngelo, Robin. "Foreword." In *Me and White Supremacy: Combat Racism, Change the World, and Become a Good Ancestor*, by Layla F. Saad, xi–xiii. Naperville, IL: Sourcebooks, 2010.

———. *White Fragility: Why It's So Hard for White People to Talk about Racism*. Boston: Beacon, 2018.

Diaz, Johnny. "Bust of Klan Leader Removed from Tennessee Capitol." *New York Times*, Jul 23, 2021. https://www.nytimes.com/2021/07/23/us/nathan-bedford-forrest-bust.html.

Dickerson, Dennis C. *The African Methodist Episcopal Church: A History*. Cambridge: Cambridge University Press, 2019.

Dreier, Peter. "The Real Story of Baseball's Integration That You Won't See in 42." *The Atlantic*, Apr 11, 2013. https://www.theatlantic.com/entertainment/archive/2013/04/the-real-story-of-baseballs-integration-that-you-wont-see-in-i-42-i/274886/.

Duncan, Lenny. *Dear Church: A Love Letter from a Black Preacher to the Whitest Denomination in the U.S.* Minneapolis: Fortress, 2019.

Dupont, Carolyn Renée. *Mississippi Praying: Southern White Evangelicals and the Civil Rights Movement, 1945–1975*. New York: New York University Press, 2013.

Emerson, Michael O., and Christian Smith. *Divided by Faith: Evangelical Religion and the Problem of Race in America*. New York: Oxford University Press, 2000.

Bibliography

Equiano, Oloudah. *The Interesting Narrative of the Life of Oloudah Equiano, or Gustavus Vassa, the African.* Chapel Hill: University of North Carolina at Chapel Hill, 2001. Orig. pub. 1789. https://faculty.uml.edu/bmarshall/The%20Interesting%20Narrative%20of%20the%20Life%20of%20Olaudah%20Equiano.pdf.

"Fair Housing Exhibit." St. Luke's UMC, n.d. https://www.stlukesumc.com/antiracist/.

Feder, Sandra. "Stanford Psychologist Identifies Seven Factors That Contribute to American Racism." *Stanford News*, Jun 9, 2020. https://news.stanford.edu/2020/06/09/seven-factors-contributing-american-racism/.

Feldman, Ella Malena. "First United Methodist Church of Austin Eliminates Debt for HBCU Huston-Tillotson Students." *Austin American-Statesman*, Aug 8, 2021. https://www.statesman.com/story/news/2021/08/08/austins-first-united-methodist-church-pays-debt-hbcu-huston-tillotson-graduates/5519616001/.

Field, David N. "John Wesley as a Public Theologian: The Case of *Thoughts upon Slavery.*" *Scriptura* 114 (2015) 1–13. https://www.academia.edu/20191812/John_Wesley_as_a_Public_Theologian_The_Case_of_Thoughts_Upon_Slavery.

Findlay, James F., Jr. *Church People in the Struggle: The National Council of Churches and the Black Freedom Movement, 1950–1970.* New York: Oxford University Press, 1991.

Forman, James. "The Black Manifesto." In *To Redeem a Nation: A History and Anthology of the Civil Rights Movement,* edited by Thomas R. West and James W. Mooney, 250–2. St. James, NY: Brandywine, 1993.

Foy, Nicole. "A Boise Church 'Repents' and Will Remove Stained-Glass Window of Confederate General Robert E. Lee." *Idaho Statesman*, Jun 12, 2020. https://www.eastidahonews.com/2020/06/a-boise-church-repents-and-will-remove-stained-glass-window-of-confederate-general-robert-e-lee/.

Garrison, William Lloyd. *Thoughts on African Colonization.* New York: Arno, 1969. Orig. pub. 1832. https://archive.org/details/thoughtsonafricaoooogarr/page/n3/mode/2up?view=theater.

George, Carol V. R. *One Mississippi, Two Mississippi: Methodists, Murder and the Struggle for Racial Justice in Neshoba County.* New York: Oxford University Press, 2015.

Gilbert, Kathy L. "United Methodists Preach, Protest and Decry Racism." *UM News*, Jun 1, 2020. https://www.umnews.org/en/news/united-methodists-preach-protest-and-decry-racism.

Graham, J. H. G. *Black United Methodists: Retrospect and Prospect.* New York: Vantage, 1979.

Gravely, William B. *Gilbert Haven: Methodist Abolitionist.* Nashville: Abingdon, 1973.

———. "Methodist Preachers, Slavery and Caste: Types of Social Concern in Antebellum America." *The Duke Divinity School Review* 34 (1969) 209–29.

Green, Linda. "United Methodists Pay Homage to African Americans Who Stayed." *UM News*, Apr 1, 2004. https://www.umnews.org/en/news/united-methodists-pay-homage-to-african-americans-who-stayed.

Hahn, Heather. "Pastors with a Badge Advance Police Reforms." *UM News*, Jul 29, 2020. https://www.umnews.org/en/news/pastors-with-a-badge-advance-police-reforms.

Hahn, Heather, and Tim Tanton. "2 Jurisdictions Tackle Racism in Bishop Elections." *UM News*, Nov 4, 2022. https://www.umnews.org/en/news/2-jurisdictions-tackle-racism-in-bishopelections.

Hahn, Heather, et al. "Jurisdictions See Shift in Bishops, More Cooperation." *UM News*, Nov 7, 2022. https://www.umnews.org/en/news/jurisdictions-see-shift-in-bishops-more-cooperation.

Bibliography

Hall, Jacquelyn Dowd. *Revolt Against Chivalry: Jessie Daniel Ames and the Women's Campaign Against Lynching.* New York: Columbia University Press, 1993.

Hannah-Jones, Nikole, et al. *The 1619 Project.* New York: One World, 2021.

Harvey, Paul. *Christianity and Race in the American South: A History.* Chicago: University of Chicago Press, 2016.

Hawkins, J. Russell. *The Bible Told Them So: How Southern Evangelicals Fought to Preserve White Supremacy.* New York: Oxford University Press, 2021.

Heinsohn, Edmund. *Fifty Years: Courtroom Pulpit.* Austin: San Felipe, 1972.

Hildebrand, Reginald F. *The Times Were Strange and Stirring: Methodist Preachers and the Crisis of Emancipation.* Durham: Duke University Press, 1995.

Jacobson, Eric S. "Silent Observer or Silent Partner: Methodism and the Texas Ku Klux Klan, 1921–1925." *Methodist History* 31 (1993) 104–12.

Jones, Clarence B., and Stuart Connelly. *Behind the Dream: The Making of the Speech That Transformed a Nation.* New York: St. Martin's, 2011.

Jones, Robert P. *White Too Long: The Legacy of White Supremacy in American Christianity.* New York: Simon & Schuster, 2020.

Keating, Ann Durkin. "Keep Up the Agitation: Rev. Jerry Forshey and a KKK Cross from Jackson, Mississippi." *Journal of the Illinois State Historical Association* 107 (2014) 45–76.

Kenaston, Connor S. "Methodists and Lynching: Racial Violence and the Methodist Episcopal Church, South, 1880–1930." *Methodist Review* 7 (2015) 21–43.

King, Martin Luther, Jr. "Letter from Birmingham Jail." *RealClear Politics*, Jan 19, 2015. Orig. pub. Jun 12, 1963. https://www.realclearpolitics.com/articles/2015/01/19/letter_from_a_birmingham_jail_125300.html#!.

———. "Our God is Marching On!" The Martin Luther King, Jr. Research and Education Institute. https://kinginstitute.stanford.edu/our-god-marching.

Kirkpatrick, Dow. "The Methodist Church [and the Race Problem]: It Reflects Culture as Much as It Reforms It." *Christianity and Crisis* 18 (1963) 26–28.

KKK 1871 Congressional Testimony. 1871. https://archive.org/details/KKK1871CongressionalTestimony/South%20Carolina%20Volume%20II/page/n527/mode/2up.

Knotts, Alice G. *Fellowship of Love: Methodist Women Changing American Racial Attitudes, 1920–1968.* Nashville: Kingswood Books, 1996.

———. "Race Relations in the 1920s: A Challenge to Southern Methodist Women." *Methodist History* 26 (1988) 199–212.

Kosek, Joseph Kip. "'Just a Bunch of Agitators': Kneel-Ins and the Desegregation of the Southern Churches." *Religion and American Culture: A Journal of Interpretation* 23 (2013) 232–61.

Kwon, Duke L., and Gregory Thompson. *Reparations: A Christian Call for Repentance and Repair.* Grand Rapids: Brazos, 2021.

Learney, Milo, and Francis Galan. *San Antonio's Churches.* Charleston: Arcadia, 2012.

Lee, Chandis Innis. "'Do No Harm': An Open Letter to the United Methodist College of Bishops of the Northeastern, Southeastern, North Central, South Central and Western Jurisdictions of the United States of America." n.d. https://docs.google.com/forms/d/e/1FAIpQLSddxPsoKOhR5HS4Y_Rddc6A1lQJYU2e6afWDBE-m6aKqqFSkw/viewform?fbclid=IwAR3L9M8iCvzav5420F7OsyxQapmd9mPZHPoRzzvEutmdxa4_HU6Mfy6nmlw.

Bibliography

LeMoult, Craig. "Some White Congregations Are Paying to Use Hymns Written by Enslaved African People." *NPR*, Jan 8, 2022. https://www.npr.org/2022/01/08/1071542936/some-white-congregations-are-paying-to-use-hymns-written-by-enslaved-african-peo.

Lord, Richard. "Church Shelters Protestors amid Deadly Turmoil." *UM News*, Apr 13, 2017. https://www.umnews.org/en/news/church-shelters-protesters-amid-deadlyturmoil.

Lynching in America: Confronting the Legacy of Racial Terror. 3rd ed. Montgomery: Equal Justice Initiative, 2017. https://lynchinginamerica.eji.org/report/.

Lyon, Carter Dalton. *Sanctuaries of Segregation: The Story of the Jackson Church Visit Campaign.* Jackson: University Press of Mississippi, 2017.

"The Making of an Era: Central Texans Reflect on the Civil Rights Movement." *Austin American-Statesman*, Apr 7, 2014. https://www.statesman.com/story/news/2014/04/07/the-making-of-an-era-central-texans-refect-on-the-civil-rights-movement/10091204007/.

Mars, Florence. *Witness in Philadelphia.* Baton Rouge: Louisiana State University Press, 1977.

Mathews, Donald G. "Orange Scott: The Methodist Evangelist as Revolutionary." In *The Antislavery Vanguard*, edited by Martin Duberman, 71–101. Princeton: Princeton University Press, 1965.

———. *Slavery and Methodism: A Chapter in American Morality, 1780–1845.* Princeton: Princeton University Press, 1965.

Matlack, Lucius C. *The History of American Slavery and Methodism from 1780 to 1849.* New York: Wesleyan Book Room Office, 1849. https://archive.org/details/ASPC0005038900.

———. *The Life of Reverend Orange Scott.* New York: C. Prindle and L. C. Matlack, 1851. https://archive.org/details/liferevorangescooscotgoog/page/n106/mode/2up?view=theater.

McClain, William B. *Black People in the Methodist Church: Whither Thou Goest?* Nashville: Abingdon, 1984.

———. "Historic Roots of Racism." The United Methodist Church, 2020. Panel discussion moderated by Erin M. Hawkins. https://www.umc.org/en/content/dismantling-racism-town-hall.

McGraw, James R. "Practice What You Print." *Christianity and Crisis* (January 1, 1968) 87–93.

McHarris, Philip V., and Thenjiwe McHarris. "No More Money for the Police." *New York Times*, May 30, 2020. https://www.nytimes.com/2020/05/30/opinion/george-floyd-police-funding.html.

McPherson, James M. *The Abolitionist Legacy: From Reconstruction to the NAACP.* Princeton: Princeton University Press, 1975.

Merger Review and Evaluation. GCORR (September 1973). GCAH.

Miller, Robert Moats. "A Note on the Relationship between the Protestant Churches and the Revived Ku Klux Klan." *The Journal of Southern History* 22 (1956) 355–68.

———. "The Protestant Churches and Lynching." *The Journal of Negro History* 42 (1957) 118–31.

Moe-Lobeda, Cynthia D. *Resisting Structural Evil: Love as Ecological-Economic Vocation.* Minneapolis: Fortress, 2013.

Bibliography

Moore-Koikoi, Cynthia. "Bishops Launch Dismantling Racism." The United Methodist Church, Jun 19, 2020. https://www.umc.org/en/content/bishops-juneteenth-dismantling-racism-announcement.

Morris-Chapman, Daniel J. Pratt. "John Wesley and the Methodist Responses to Slavery in America." *Holiness* 5 (2019) 37–58.

Murray, Peter C. *Methodists and the Crucible of Race 1930–1975*. Columbia: University of Missouri Press, 2004.

Natanson, Hannah. "Are Confederate Monument Fans Committing the Sin of Idol Worship? An Unusual Charlottesville Bible Study Makes the Case." *Washington Post*, Sep 13, 2019. https://www.washingtonpost.com/religion/2019/09/13/are-confederate-monument-fans-committing-sin-idol-worship-an-unusual-charlottesville-bible-study-makes-case/.

Newman, Richard. *Freedom's Prophet: Bishop Richard Allen, the AME Church, and the Black Founding Fathers*. New York: New York University Press, 2008.

Nicholas, William E. *Go and Be Reconciled: Alabama Methodists Confront Racism, 1954–1974*. Montgomery: NewSouth, 2018.

"Night Call: Building Understanding and Reconciliation through Conversation." The United Methodist Church, n.d. https://www.umc.org/en/content/night-call.

Noll, Mark A. *The Civil War as a Theological Crisis*. Chapel Hill: University of North Carolina Press, 2006.

Norwood, Frederick. *The Story of American Methodism*. Nashville: Abingdon, 1974.

Norwood, John. *The Schism in the Methodist Episcopal Church: 1844*. New York: Alfred, 1923.

Oluo, Ijeoma. *So You Want to Talk about Race*. New York: Hachette, 2019.

Outler, Albert C., ed. *John Wesley*. Oxford: Oxford University Press, 1964.

Painter, Kyle. "The Pro-Slavery Argument in the Development of the American Methodist Church." *Constructing the Past* 2 (2001) 29–46.

Patterson, Jim. "Smaller Communities Affected by Protests." *UM News*, Jul 9, 2020. https://www.umnews.org/en/news/smaller-communities-affected-by-protests.

———. "Striving for Equity in Pastor Salaries." *UM News*, Jun 16, 2022. https://www.umnews.org/en/news/striving-for-equity-in-pastor-salaries.

———. "Virginia Church Contemplates Racism in the Ranks." *UM News*, Apr 7, 2021. https://www.umnews.org/en/news/virginia-church-contemplates-racism-in-the-ranks.

———. "White Church Donates to Reparations Fund." *UM News*, Mar 14, 2022. https://www.umnews.org/en/news/white-church-donates-to-reparations-fund.

Phipps, William E. "John Wesley on Slavery." *Quarterly Review* 1 (1981) 23–31.

Pinar, William F. *The Gender of Racial Politics and Violence in America: Lynching, Prison Rape and the Crisis of Masculinity*. Frankfurt: Peter Lang, 2001.

"Racial Justice." The United Methodist Church, n.d. https://www.umc.org/en/how-we-serve/advocating-for-justice/racial-justice.

"Racial Justice." United Women in Faith, n.d. https://uwfaith.org/what-we-do/serve-and-advocate/racial-justice/.

"Racial Justice Backed." *United Methodist Reporter* (May 2, 1980). GCAH.

"Racial Justice Time Line: Important Moments of Racial Justice History in the United States and United Methodist Women." The North Texas Conference of the United Methodist Church, n.d. https://ntcumc.org/UMW_RJtimeline.pdf.

Bibliography

"Racism in Programs." GCORR (1980). GCAH.

"Racism in Rural Areas Task Force Report." *Daily Christian Advance* (1996) 849–67. GCAH.

Rambin, James. "When the Klan Took Republic Square." *Towers*, Dec 17, 2019. https://austin.towers.net/when-the-klan-took-republic-square/.

Rasmus, Rudy, ed. *I'm Black. I'm Christian. I'm Methodist.* Nashville: Abingdon, 2020.

Reiff, Joseph T. *Born of Conviction: White Methodists and Mississippi's Closed Society.* New York: Oxford University Press, 2016.

Richey, Russell E., et al. *American Methodism: A Compact History.* Nashville: Abingdon, 2010.

———. *The Methodist Experience in America.* 2 vols. 1st ed. Nashville: Abingdon, 2010.

———. *The Methodist Experience in America.* 2 vols. 2nd ed. Nashville: Abingdon, 2020.

Ross, Bobby, Jr. "Tulsa Race Massacre Prayer Room Highlights Churches' 1921 Sins, Seeks Healing." *Religion Unplugged*, May 26, 2021. https://religionunplugged.com/news/2021/5/26/tulsa-race-massacre-prayer-room-highlights-churches-1921-sins-seeks-healing.

Saad, Layla F. *Me and White Supremacy.* Naperville, IL: Sourcebooks, 2010.

Sabree, Rahkim. "Racism and White Supremacy." *Medium*, Jun 7, 2022. https://medium.com/ifiredmyboss/racism-and-white-supremacy-3a500357bbb7.

Schneider, Gregory S. "Richmond Takes Down Its Last Major City-Owned Confederate Memorial." *Washington Post*, Dec 12, 2022. https://www.washingtonpost.com/dc-md-va/2022/12/12/richmond-confederate-statue-hill-removal/.

Shankman, Arnold. "Dorothy Tilly, Civil Rights, and the Methodist Church." *Methodist History* 18 (1980) 95–108.

Shattuck, Gardiner H., Jr. *Episcopalians and Race: Civil War to Civil Rights.* Lexington: University Press of Kentucky, 2000.

Smith, Clint. *How the Word Is Passed: A Reckoning with the History of Slavery across America.* New York: Little, Brown and Company, 2021.

Smith, Warren Thomas. *John Wesley and Slavery.* Nashville: Abingdon, 1986.

"Statement by Alabama Clergymen." The Martin Luther King, Jr. Research and Education Institute, n.d. Orig. pub. 1963. https://kinginstitute.stanford.edu/sites/mlk/files/lesson-activities/clergybirmingham1963.pdf.

"Statement from the Administrative Board." Mt. Zion United Methodist Church, July 2, 2020. https://myemail.constantcontact.com/Mid-Week-at-Mt—Zion.html?soid=11 10219398180&aid=hlHaQ7ru WlY.

Steps Toward Wholeness: Learning and Repentance. Prepared by the UMC General Commission on Christian Unity and Interreligious Concerns for the 2000 General Conference. GCAH.

Stevens, Thelma. *Legacy for the Future: The History of Christian Social Relations in the Women's Division of Christian Service, 1940–1968.* Women's Division of the Board of Global Ministries, The United Methodist Church, 1978.

Stovall, Denise Johnson. "Delegates Call on Entire Church for Riot-Aftermath Compassion." *United Methodist Reporter* (May 15, 1992) 1–2. GCAH.

Straker, Ian. "Black and White and Gray All Over: Freeborn Garrettson and African Methodism." *Methodist History* 37.1 (1998) 18–27.

———. "The Central Jurisdiction." *Methodist History* 54 (2015) 37–70.

Bibliography

———. "Embracing the Whole Truth about Methodism and Race." *United Methodist Insight,* Sep 9, 2020. https://um-insight.net/perspectives/embracing-whole-truth-about-methodism-and-race/.

———. "Non-Merging Streams: The Continuing Problem of Race in American Methodism." *Methodist History* 57 (October 2018 and January 2019) 96–110.

Sugrue, Thomas J. *Sweet Land of Liberty: The Forgotten Struggle for Civil Rights in the North.* New York: Random House, 2008.

"Take Action: Police Reform," Church & Society, n.d. https://www.umcjustice.org/articles/take-action-police-reform-1061.

Thomas, James S. *Methodism's Racial Dilemma: The Story of the Central Jurisdiction.* Nashville: Abingdon, 1992.

Tisby, Jemar. *The Color of Compromise: The Truth about the American Church's Complicity in Racism.* Grand Rapids: Zondervan, 2019.

———. *How to Fight Racism: Courageous Christianity and the Journey toward Racial Justice.* Grand Rapids: Zondervan, 2021.

Tocqueville, Alexis de. *Democracy in America.* Translated by Arthur Goldhammer. The Library of America, 2004. Orig. pub. 1835.

"Tulsa's Race Riot and the Teachings of Jesus." *The Christian Advocate* (July 1921) 911–913. https://www.tulsahistory.org/wp-content/uploads/2018/11/E-D-Mouzon_Tulsa-Race-Riot-Sermon_Christian-Advocate-07141921_and-transcription-00000003.pdf.

Vernon, Walter N., et al. *The Methodist Excitement in Texas: A History.* Dallas: Texas United Methodist Historical Society, 1984.

Wesley, John. *Hymns and Sacred Poems.* Duke Divinity School, n.d. Orig. pub. 1739. https://divinity.duke.edu/sites/divinity.duke.edu/files/documents/cswt/04_Hymns_and_Sacred_Poems_(1739).pdf.

———. "Thoughts upon Slavery." In *The Works of John Wesley,* vol. 11, edited by Thomas Jackson, 59–79. Grand Rapids: Zondervan, 1958.

"The Western North Carolina Conference Calls for the Removal of Confederate Monument Adjacent to Mt. Zion United Methodist Church." Western North Carolina Conference, Jul 6, 2020. https://www.wnccumc.org/newsdetail/wncc-extended-cabinet-calls-for-removal-of-confederate-monument-14120797.

Whisnant, Miriam Smith. *The History of Mount Zion United Methodist Church.* Cornelius, NC: Mount Zion United Methodist Church, 1978. https://archive.org/details/mountzionunitedmoomoun/mode/2up?view=theater&q=monument.

White, Deborah. "Leaders Remember Central Jurisdiction's Dissolution." *UM News,* Apr 27, 2008. https://www.umnews.org/en/news/leaders-remember-central-jurisdictions-dissolution.

White, Marie S. "The Antislavery Struggle in the Land of Lincoln." *Methodist History* 10 (1972) 33–52.

White, Woodie. "Do We Really Believe in Open Pulpits?" *Circuit Rider* (January 1978). GCAH.

———. "Racism: The Church's Unfinished Agenda." In *A Journal of the National United Methodist Church on Racism,* edited by Kelley Fitzgerald (September 1987). GCAH.

"Who We Are." St. Luke's UMC, n.d. https://www.stlukesumc.com/who-we-are.

Wilkerson, Isabel. *Caste: The Origins of Our Discontents.* New York: Random House, 2020.

———. *The Warmth of Other Suns: The Epic Story of America's Great Migration.* New York: Random House, 2010.

Bibliography

Willimon, Will. *Who Lynched Willie Earl? Preaching to Confront Racism.* Nashville: Abingdon, 2017.

Wise, Tim. "Tim Wise's Definitions." Tools for Racial Justice, n.d. https://tools4racialjustice. net/tim-wises-definitions/.

Wood, Forrest G. *The Arrogance of Faith: Christianity and Race in America.* New York: Knopf, 1990.

Worth, J. Mark. "The Moral Arc of the Universe." Harvard Unitarian Universalist Church, Nov 13, 2016. https://uuharvard.org/services/moral-arc-of-the-universe/.

Index

Index

Index

race riots, 28, 60–62, 73, 85, 94

racial justice, 122; "Charter for Racial Justice," 118; GCORR on, 117; Lawson, James, on 85; local church teams and, 62, 138–39, 141–42, 144, 146, 149, 155; Methodist women on, 110–11, 123; obstacles to, 113, 149–50, 156; practices, 131–32; resistance to, 123–29

racial reconciliation, 36, 62, 156; "Act of Repentance" for, 120–21; in early abolitionism, 36; Fund for, 85, 117; in police reform, 141

racism: in baseball, 108; and the CJ, 69–72, 81, 121; colorblindness and, 127–29; definition of, 2–5; dismantling of, 6–8, 85, 104–5, 112, 122, 131–32, 152–57; Forman, James, on, 116; GCORR on, 85, 115, 119; local church and, 118, 126, 137–38, 149; in the MEC, 121; MFSA on, 92; Methodist women on, 108–10, 112, 123, 150–51; police reform and, 140–42; repentance of, 120–21; rural areas and, 120; *Social Principles*, 117; systemic, 2, 4–5, 21, 47, 72–74, 85–86, 113, 124, 126, 154

racism index (PRRI), 124

Reconstruction, 49–51

reparations, 143–46

Rickey, Branch, 107–8

Robinson, Jackie, 107–8

Satterfield, John, 84, 89

school desegregation, Auburn University, 105–6

Scott, Orange, 36–38

Second Methodist Conference on Human Relations, 104

segregation: AMML, 80; CJ and, 71–72; in the church, 32, 49, 77–85, 99–103; in education, 52–53;

Haven, Gilbert, 54; MAMML, 93; MEC and, 55, 73–74; MECS and, 63; in the North, 57, 72–73; Methodist institutions, 85–88; Methodist women on, 79, 108–12; spirituality of the church, 55, 74; theological worldview of, 88–90

Selah, W.B., 96, 101

Slavery. *See* enslaved persons

slave trade, 13–14, 58

Social Creed, 92–93, 108

Social Principles, 117, 143

Stevens, Thelma, 108–10

St. George's Methodist Church (Philadelphia, PA), 31

"Thoughts Upon Slavery" (Wesley), 13–19

Tilly, Dorothy, 109

Tisby, Jemar, 3, 10, 34, 48, 74, 129, 142

Tittle, Ernest Freemont, 145

Tougaloo College (Jackson, MS), 99–102

Tulsa Massacre, 60–62

Turnipseed, Marti, 106

University UMC (Austin, TX), xi, xii, 9, 141–42, 145–49

voluntarism, 80–81

Wesley, Charles, 12

Wesley, John, 12–20, 24, 26; on abolition, 19; antislavery stance, 20–22; general rule against slavery, 135; theology of, 20–22

Wesleyan Methodist Connection, 38

White, Woodie, 115, 119

White Citizens' Councils, 90–91, 93, 100, 137, 147

Whitefield, George, 22–24

White Supremacy, 5, 48

Wofford College (Spartanburg, SC), 87–88

Made in United States
Troutdale, OR
08/21/2024

22210778R00106